MW01445906

DENIS JENKINSON
A PASSION FOR PORSCHES

Dr Ferry Porsche, the head of the present family.

DENIS JENKINSON
A PASSION FOR PORSCHES

A RE-ISSUE OF THE CLASSIC
PORSCHE PAST & PRESENT
The author's personal memories
of his favourite marque

Haynes Publishing

© Denis Jenkinson Estate

All rights reserved. No part of this publication may be reproduced, stored in a retrieval system or transmitted, in any form or by any means, electronic, mechanical, photocopying, recording or otherwise, without prior permission in writing from the publisher.

First published in 1983 by Gentry Books Ltd as *Porsche Past & Present*
Re-issued in 2001 by Haynes Publishing as *A Passion for Porsches*
Reprinted in 2004

A catalogue record for this book is available from the British Library

ISBN 1 85960 815 9

Library of Congress catalog card no. 00-136566

Haynes North America Inc., 861 Lawrence Drive, Newbury Park, California 91320, USA.

Published by Haynes Publishing,
Sparkford, Yeovil, Somerset BA22 7JJ, UK.
Tel: 01963 442030 Fax: 01963 440001
Int.tel: +44 1963 442030 Fax: +44 1963 440001
E-mail: sales@haynes.co.uk
Web site: www.haynes.co.uk

Printed and bound in Britain by J.H. Haynes & Co. Ltd., Sparkford

Contents

Preface to the 2001 re-issue by Doug Nye
page 9

Chapter
ONE
The P-Wagen
Dr Porsche: P-Wagen: Auto Union: Bernd Rosemeyer: Volkswagen:
page 13

Chapter
TWO
Origins
Berlin-Rome: Porsche VW: First Porsche: Motorcycle racing: AFN:
page 22

Chapter
THREE
Indoctrination
Aprilia: Richard von Frankenberg: Michael Burn: Dr Harrison:
page 29

Chapter
FOUR
Joining the family
Passport to anywhere: Factory racing: Pride: Souvenirs:
page 35

Chapter
FIVE
Friends
Jesse Alexander: Peter Coltrin: Steve Wilder: Jack Burke: Jim Clark:
page 45

Chapter
SIX
The Carrera
The origin: AFN Ltd: Private owner: Factory cars:
page 58

Chapter
SEVEN
Competitions
Sprints and Hill Climbs: Six Hours Relay: Lightweight: Performance:
page 67

Chapter
EIGHT
The Targa Florio
The race: RS60: Carrera: Long distances: Graham Hill: 908/3:
page 79

Chapter
NINE
Porsche over Europe
To Sicily: Messina ferry: Sicily: Austria: Portugal: Germany:
page 91

Chapter
TEN
Brief encounters
Arctic Circle: Lost Porsche: Formula 2:
page 106

Chapter
ELEVEN
Of the Porsche kind
RSK: 904 and the cake: GT40: 935 Turbo:
page 120

Chapter
TWELVE
Owner's troubles
Wilder's Crash: A car wash: Clutch cables: Windscreen: Engine:
page 132

Chapter
THIRTEEN
A New Generation
911 Prototype: Road Tests: Sportomatic: 914:
page 145

Chapter
FOURTEEN
The 911 grows up
The 911S: The 2.7-litre: The Turbo: The 3.3 Turbo:
page 159

Chapter
FIFTEEN
The 917
Rumours: Bombshell: Testing: Can-Am: Weissach:
page 170

Chapter
SIXTEEN
Another World
Front engines: Water cooling: The 924: 928: 944:
page 184

Chapter
SEVENTEEN
Porsche today
Weissach: Racing: Le Mans 1982: Formula One:
page 197

Index
page 203

Preface to the 2001 re-issue

by Doug Nye

Denis Jenkinson was, to several generations of motor sport enthusiasts, the best-connected, most influential and most accurate journalistic observer of the international scene. Known universally as 'Jenks', he was far more than 'just' a motor racing journalist. Indeed, he never cared to be described as any such thing – except on his passport and tax return – preferring instead to call himself, quite simply, 'an enthusiast'.

And that he most decidedly was. Ever since his youth as an almost obsessively nit-picking reader of the British magazines *The Autocar*, *The Motor* and *Motor Sport*, Jenks consciously committed himself to 'the motor racing life'. Chance saw him enjoy his baptism as a go-for mechanic on Bob Cowell's sports Alta at Brooklands in 1939, and after the war years – spent as a technician at the Royal Aircraft Establishment, Farnborough – he quickly established himself as a critical observer and sometime participant within British, then European, motor sport.

He drove his sports Frazer Nash in the first British post-war race meeting – at Gransden Lodge – but couldn't afford to keep it, so blew £100 of the proceeds on a 350cc Norton racing motorcycle. Packing all his worldly goods onto it, he took off to the Continent for 1948, pursuing the gypsy life of a racing motorcyclist. Then, after blowing up his solo's precious engine, he volunteered himself as passenger for sidecar racer Eric Oliver. The rugged veteran rider sized up bearded, diminutive Jenks, gave him a test ride at Floreffe in Belgium and recognised an entirely fearless kindred spirit. Together in 1949 they became motorcycling's inaugural Sidecar World Champions.

Jenks supplemented his meagre earnings by sending home written race reports and columns for *Motor-Cycling*, *The News Chronicle*, *Iota* and *Motor Sport*. He rode with Belgian Marcel Masuy from 1950 to 1952, based in Brussels, but on 11 March 1953, Wesley Tee – owner of *Motor Sport* – offered him an exclusive freelance arrangement as Continental Correspondent, and he took it.

A Passion for Porsches

From then through to the 1990s, Jenks and 'The Bod' – Bill Boddy, his editor – 'were' *Motor Sport*. Their work, avidly consumed in the late 1950s and early 1960s by some 160,000 buyers of this monthly magazine, shaped and informed generations of enthusiasts throughout the English-speaking world. Jenks was liked, respected and above all trusted by racing people, on two wheels and four, despite his often controversial opinions, fearlessly – and loudly – expressed. He might sometimes have been wrong, but was regarded as utterly incorruptible.

In 1954 Jenks navigated George Abecassis in an HWM-Jaguar in the world's leading sports car classic – the Italian Mille Miglia. For the 1955 race Stirling Moss recruited him to navigate his works Mercedes-Benz 300SLR. They won! Moss and Jenks contested two more Mille Miglia races – 1956 and 1957 – for Maserati, and when Stirling fought Mike Hawthorn hard for the Formula 1 World Championship in 1958, Jenks (no mere reporter) often kept the Vanwall team's lap charts.

He was always, in his own right, a keen and perceptive driver. When Tee offered to buy him a 'decent' company car for his journeys on *Motor Sport*'s behalf, Jenks specified a Porsche 356. His experience of it was the start of a love affair with Porsche and Porsche people – and with the post-war AFN company which, before the war, had built the Frazer Nash he had once so adored. The relationship lasted virtually to the day Jenks died, 29 November 1996.

His was an almost matchless enthusiasm, an all-absorbing obsession with the best of mechanical magic. His self-penned obituary ended with the line, 'A product of the 20th century, he enjoyed and wondered at it all his life'. Typically, nobody could have put it better, and most notably he recognised similar qualities in the people at Porsche and admired their products and loved them for it.

Royalties from the sales of this re-issued classic are to be donated to BEN – the Motor & Allied Trades Benevolent Fund – in whose Sunningdale home Jenks spent his final days, among friends who kept him in comfort and cared for him with respect and affection, as they have done for many thousands of motor industry veterans and their families.

Jenks with Doug Nye, focusing no doubt on weighty matters (Geoff Goddard).

Acknowledgements

It is always difficult to decide who should be acknowledged when you have finished writing a book such as this, for it spans nearly 50 years of interest in the effects of Professor Ferdinand Porsche on the automotive world. If anyone should be acknowledged it should be the venerable old gentleman who started the whole world of Porsche engineering, and also his brilliant son Dr Ferry Porsche who continued his father's work and built up the Porsche empire from the shreds left after the war in 1945.

In the span of years from Auto Union 'P-Wagen' to Porsche 944, I have 'talked cars' to people all over the world and particularly to Porsche enthusiasts, all far too numerous to mention by name. Most of those who aided and abetted me in my Porsche motoring are mentioned in the text; some are sadly no longer with us, like Jack Burke, Tommy Pascoe, Peter Coltrin, Richard von Frankenberg, Jean Behra and Jimmy Clark – while Hubert Mimmler died very recently. Others are still on the motoring scene and enjoy reminiscing about 'old Porsche days' or discuss today's Porsche cars and the firm's racing activity, right up to winning the 1982 Endurance Championship. Steve Wilder, Jesse Alexander, Sandy Burnett, Michael Burn and others feature strongly in the formative years. Today my thanks must go to friends like Jerry Sloniger, Geoff Goddard, Michael Cotton and Delwyn Mallett who helped me with obscure photographs needed to illustrate many small, but important points in the story.

Members of the Aldington family and AFN Ltd must all feature on this page, for without them my Porsche activity would have been very limited; so many thanks to H. J. (Aldy) who helped with the acquisition of my 356A, and W. H. (Uncle Bill) who kept lending me cars and J. T. A. (young John) who is now in charge of Porsche Cars Great Britain Ltd. My grateful acknowledgements to members of the Porsche Club in countries around the world, who are always happy to 'talk Porsche,' and to members of the Porsche Club of Great Britain who keep the Stuttgart-Zuffenhausen flag flying in the UK and perpetuate the feeling of being in the Porsche family.

Foreword

Nobody will dispute the fact that the firm of Dr.Ing.h.c.F.Porsche KG of Stuttgart-Zuffenhausen is one of the world's most important car manufacturers, not the largest and not the most successful financially, but in the world of automotive engineering certainly one of the most respected. From its inception in 1948 the firm, started and developed by Ferry Porsche, has made racing one of its main reasons for being in existence and through racing successes the name Porsche has grown up to be respected throughout the world. I was fortunate in being around at the time of those early beginnings and was instantly attracted to this new style of sports car, with its streamlined coupé body and very soon fell under the spell of these little 356 'beetle' cars, designed and built round Volkswagen components.

I soon found that Porsche was a way of life and Porsche motoring was something rather special, and in this book I have recounted many of the happenings during those early years of the company's expansion, not from a company history point of view, but through the eyes of a Porsche user and an enthusiast for racing. At the same time Porsche engineering skill was breaking new ground, and setting new standards by which to judge anything and everything so that Porsche Engineering were two words that became important in my vocabulary.

Although I have not had the ownership experience of Porsches like many people I know, I have driven most models and have followed the racing activities of the firm closely. Indeed, I am looking forward with interest and excitement to the appearance of the new Porsche engine in Formula One Grand Prix racing. I became a Porsche believer in 1950 when I first rode in a 356 and still get the same satisfying feeling when I drive the latest 944. There is something extraordinarily exciting about a Porsche and I hope this book will instil some of that feeling to non-believers, if they take the trouble to read it. For Porsche enthusiasts I can only 'preach to the converted', and many will be greater fans of everything that Dr. Porsche's name stands for than I am. Even so I hope they will enjoy my tales of Porsche past and present.

Crondall, Hampshire   Denis Jenkinson

Chapter ONE

The P-Wagen

I first became aware of Dr Ferdinand Porsche, later to become Professor, while I was still at school, though at the time there was not a Porsche car as such. My schoolboy passion was Grand Prix racing, and for that matter it still is, so when a new Grand Prix Formula was proposed for the years 1934, 1935 and 1936 I looked forward with keen interest. Alfa Romeo, Bugatti and Maserati were the leading makes in Grand Prix racing at the time and they were obviously going to continue into the era of the new Formula, but excitement ran high with the knowledge that Daimler-Benz were preparing a team of Mercedes-Benz racing cars, and that a new automobile combine, called Auto Union, were building a car for the new Formula. Auto Union, spelt with a hyphen or without to choice it seems, was a combination of four firms and their badge comprised four inter-linked rings across the name Auto Union, each ring representing one of the members of the consortium. They were Audi, DKW, Horch and Wanderer, all engineering and vehicle manufacturers of known standing and ability. The first news of their new Grand Prix car was that it was to be called the *P-wagen* (*wagen* being German for car).

It was quite a time before any photographs were released of the Auto Union *P-wagen*, and when they were it was seen to be a revolutionary design for the period, with the driver sitting well forward and the engine mounted behind him, with the gearbox out behind the rear axle. Today this is the normal layout for any racing car, but remember that we are talking about 1933/4 when racing cars had a distinctive radiator at the front, a long bonnet covering the engine, and the driver sitting near the rear axle, with fuel carried

A Passion for Porsches

in a pointed tail-tank. This *P-wagen* was fascinating, the more so because of its designation: in those days, any 'foreign' words connected with Grand Prix racing added allure. Words like *tribune – ravittaillement – rennabteilung – scuderia* and so on, put the pure Grand Prix racing enthusiast in England a cut above mere motoring enthusiasts. Consequently, to talk knowledgeably about the new *P-wagen* was to be one-up on people who knew only about MG or Riley cars. Little did I know what the P stood for, and even less that it was going to become such a large part of my motoring life in the years to come.

This mysterious *P-wagen*, only called this because the management could not think of a more reasonable name and had yet to commit the group name Auto Union to an individual car, was bristling with new ideas: independent front suspension by torsion bars, a single large fuel tank mounted in the centre of the car, between the driver and the engine, a 5-speed gearbox, swing-axle rear suspension and a V16-cylinder engine that was full of interest. With the engine coupled directly to the gearbox/rear-axle assembly, there was no propeller shaft and with the driver sitting forward of all the mechanical components his seat was incredibly low, which allowed the whole bodywork to be low and compact. It was an exciting and menacing-looking car to me, almost evil in some ways, and fully justified the mysterious *P-wagen* name.

It was some while before I learnt that the P in the name stood for Porsche and that it had been designed by Dr Ferdinand Porsche in his studios in Stuttgart. Auto Union bought the design from him and manufactured the cars in their factories in Chemnitz and Zwickau, in what is today the East Zone of Germany. To a schoolboy the names of these far-eastern German towns added to the excitement of this new make in Grand Prix racing. I was used to Molsheim, Milan, Bologna and Stuttgart, even if I did not really know where they were, but Chemnitz and Zwickau I had never even heard of. They certainly did not come into my geography lessons at school, more's the pity. Dr Porsche had worked for Austro-Daimler, Benz and Daimler-Benz and had been a pupil of Dr Rumpler who had designed a rear-engined Benz racing car in 1923. After leaving the Daimler-Benz company, where he had been

The Auto Union badge, showing the four inter-linked rings, each one representing one arm of the four-company consortium (author).

The P-Wagen

An Auto Union racing car seen at the Montlhéry track with Dr Porsche standing behind it. The fact that the car carried the Nazi swastika was really no more significant than a Bentley carrying a Union Jack (Porsche GB Ltd).

responsible for the mighty SS and SSK Mercedes-Benz cars from the Stuttgart firm, Dr Porsche set himself up as an independent design consultant, with drawing offices in Stuttgart, and had actually planned the V16 *P-wagen* long before Auto Union decided to go racing.

I followed the fortunes of the Auto Union team avidly for I thought it was the most sensational and exciting Grand Prix car of all time. I had been an Alfa Romeo fan until this time, and when a new young star appeared in the driving firmament in 1935, to drive the Auto Union to victory, he added to my enthusiasm for the Auto Union team. This was Bernd Rosemeyer, a handsome and dashing young German of pure Aryan stock. He had previously raced DKW motorcycles and the Auto Union was the first racing car he tried. Being totally different from any other Grand Prix car of the time, it needed a new technique to get the best from it, and Rosemeyer was the ideal man, for he had no preconceived ideas of how a racing car should feel or how he should conduct it. He was as spectacular and skilful as Gilles Villeneuve was in the 1980s, and 1936 was a glory year. Rosemeyer was

A Passion for Porsches

Dr Ferdinand Porsche in characteristic pose in front of the pits at Berne, in Switzerland, with two stop-watches 'at the ready' (Porsche Archives).

The P-Wagen

Dr Ferry Porsche is seen alongside a bronze bust of his illustrious father, Professor Ferdinand Porsche. Ferry inherited much of his father's genius for engineering and guided the family fortunes in car manufacture from the humble beginnings in Austria to the giant enterprise that it is today (Porsche Archives).

almost unbeatable with the Auto Union and his fighting spirit and audacious driving triumphed over the establishment in an impressive manner. He was my hero. When the Grand Prix Formula was extended for another year, into 1937, the V16 Auto Union continued to be a major force in the racing. Dr Porsche was 62 years' old at this time. He was a small, stout man, usually wearing a suit with a waistcoat and watch and chain, while in the pits at the races he invariably wore a trilby hat. He was essentially a serious engineer from the pioneer days. I don't think I have ever seen a photograph of him laughing: just occasionally there would be a flicker of a smile of contentment,

A Passion for Porsches

The page in the author's 1937 Grand Prix scrap-book, with the autograph of Bernd Rosemeyer alongside his photograph (G. Goddard).

but no more. He was not severe: exacting, yes, but more of a benevolent 'uncle'. A nice old boy.

Regrettably I never saw a V16 Auto Union in action, for though the team came to the 1937 Donington Park Grand Prix, and Rosemeyer won it, I was unable to get there. However, I did see the winning car, for it was put on display in the Auto Union showrooms in Great Portland Street in London, after the race. I was at technical college by this time, not far from Great Portland Street which was the home of the car trade in those days, and every lunch time for a week I walked up to the Auto Union showrooms and drooled over Dr Porsche's masterpiece. On one glorious occasion there was a group of people behind the car and I recognized my hero, Bernd Rosemeyer. Nervously, I entered the showrooms and asked him for his autograph, not in my Grand Prix scrap-book unfortunately, as I did not have it with me, but on a page in a note book. With a charming smile, he wrote his name and my joy was unbounded. As soon as I got home that evening the page was cut out and stuck in my scrap-book in which I had photos of all the Grand Prix drivers and lists of all their successes. That scrap-book is still in my library today and Rosemeyer's autograph is still there. Although I do not recall it now, I have no doubt that Dr Porsche was in that group of dignitaries in the showrooms, but I was totally star-struck by seeing Bernd Rosemeyer and did not have eyes for anyone else.

I did see the new 3-litre Auto Union V12 cars in action, at the Donington Grand Prix in 1938. However, they were nothing like the *P-wagen*, and

The P-Wagen

Rosemeyer had been killed earlier that year during a record attempt on the Frankfurt-Darmstadt Autobahn, so it was not the team it had been in my estimation. Tazio Nuvolari, the Italian Alfa Romeo 'ace', now drove for Auto Union and he won the 1938 Donington Grand Prix for the new team. Once again, the winning car appeared in the Great Portland Street showrooms, and as I was still at technical college I went armed with a camera this time, borrowed from my elder brother. It is to my permanent regret that I did not have a camera in 1937.

Dr Porsche had left the team as he had a big programme of work in hand in connection with Hitler's 'strength through joy' People's Car, or Volkswagen. The German government had chosen Dr Porsche's design from among many and he was the project engineer for the beginnings of the mighty empire at Wolfsberg that was to become Volkswagen, known after the war as 'Hitler's revenge'. It was the Volkswagen design that was to lead Dr

The simple but touching memorial erected in memory of Bernd Rosemeyer after he was killed attempting records with an Auto Union in 1938. It stands in a clearing just off the Autobahn Frankfurt-Darmstadt and is still maintained with loving care by local motor club enthusiasts (author).

The photograph of the Auto Union that the author took in the Great Portland Street showrooms in 1938, using his brother's camera (author).

The start of it all. A Volkswagen 'beetle'. This was an early post-war car with left-hand drive that the author 'drove into the ground' in the 1960s (G. Goddard).

The P-Wagen

Porsche and his son Ferry into the world of manufacturing cars carrying their family name, without which this book would not have come into being. Such small quirks of fate control one's destiny. If Auto Union had designed their own Grand Prix car in 1933, instead of taking the *P-wagen* design, I might never have become a Porsche fan. If Hitler had chosen for his People's Car a design from NSU or Daimler-Benz instead of from Porsche, the Porsche firm might never have come into being. It is the small things in life that I find so fascinating. A small decision, or a small action can affect the whole direction in which one is unconsciously travelling through life.

Chapter TWO

Origins

The Italians have always been noted for their ingenuity when it comes to motor racing and have never been short of adventurous ideas. They were the first to break the French monopoly on the Grand Prix events, when they created the Italian Grand Prix in 1921; they created the fantastic 1,000-mile race round Italy called the Mille Miglia; they built a high-speed banked track in the mid-1950s to try to encourage American-type oval-track racing in Europe, and today they have managed to get two Italian races into the World Championship calendar of Formula One events. In 1938 the Italian government put a stop to the Mille Miglia, after a series of bad accidents, so in 1939 another long-distance event was organized in Libya, from Tobruk to Tripoli, and it was planned to hold a rally, that would have become a race, from Rome to Berlin in September 1939. This was to tie in with the Italo-German political pact formed between Mussolini and Hitler, whereby the Fascist regime and the Nazi regime were to become partners against the democracies of the world. A race between the two capital cities of the partners seemed a good idea, though there was some dissention over the direction in which it should be run. Mussolini thought it should start in Berlin and finish in Rome, but Hitler had other ideas and thought the finish should be in Berlin. As things turned out, the Germans got involved in a war with France and England and the event never took place, and so, depending on your political views, you can refer to it as the Rome-Berlin race or the Berlin-Rome race.

Its point in our story is that it was the cause of the first competition car to be built from Volkswagen components carrying the stamp of Porsche, and

The 1939 Rome-Berlin streamlined Volkswagen built by Prof Porsche and his son for the marathon event that was cancelled. It is seen in action at a recent historic event at the Nurburgring and shows clearly the origins of the 356 Porsche (Delwyn Mallett).

would have been the first competitive event of a Porsche car as they would become known. As it turned out, we had to wait another eight years before that happened. Although Dr Ferdinand Porsche, who had now been awarded the honorary title of Professor, by the Third Reich, was very busy with military projects and the Volkswagen plant, his thoughts were still on motor racing and he designed and built three special coupés for the proposed Axis race. They were based on Volkswagen components, using the VW platform chassis, torsion bar suspension and rear-mounted air-cooled flat-4-cylinder engine. The streamlined body was very small and of almost single-seater proportions, and though the engine was of only 1,100cc it had a speed of nearly 90mph. As the first part of this proposed race was going to be on Autobahnen from Berlin to Munich, a high cruising speed would be essential, which could be aided by a well streamlined closed coupé body. These three cars were the forerunner of the true Porsche car though whether the good doctor had this in mind at the time is not known for sure. By this time his son Ferry was a fully qualified engineer and was working for his father's design studio. He demonstrated an obvious flair for engineering, following closely in his father's footsteps. Consequently, it was no surprise that when the first

A Passion for Porsches

Porsche coupé appeared in 1948 it looked very similar to the Berlin-Rome racing coupés.

In passing, it is worth noting that the three coupés were stored in Stuttgart during the war, during which time one of them disappeared. Of the other two, one was used by the invading American forces and finally broken up, and the third one was spirited away and saved by Otto Mathe, an Austrian racing driver, who owns it to this day.

The war years saw Professor Porsche employed by the German government on military projects and immediately afterwards the French authorities interned him due to his having done this war work. He was 70 years old when they condemned him to prison and his health was failing. His family re-established themselves in Austria and his son Ferry began work on a production car bearing their name. The prototype was an open two-seater sports car based on the Volkswagen, but this soon gave way to a small streamlined coupé that was to become known as the 356, this being the design study number. When Ferdinand Porsche had opened his design studio at the end of 1930, he had told his draughtsmen to number all their design projects and to start with number 7. He did this as he thought that no outside firm from whom he was seeking work would want a project designated 'design project number 1'. Starting at number 7 would suggest to people that the firm of 'Dr ing hc Ferdinand Porsche GmbH, Konstruktionsburo für Motoren und Fahrzeugbau' (design office for engine and motor vehicle construction) was already well established. To this day Porsche design projects have continued the original number series, the successful Le Mans 24 Hour Race winner of 1982 being design project 956.

Although first announced in the late summer of 1948, the first Porsche coupé was not seen by the public until the spring of 1949 when the firm took a stand at the Geneva Motor Show, and it was the following year when the 356 coupé began real production. The firm had now moved back to Stuttgart and the French authorities had at last released Professor Ferdinand, enabling him to rejoin his family. Naturally he was delighted with the work his son and his colleagues had done and his 75th birthday was celebrated by a gathering of Porsche owners. They were then building eight to ten cars a month. It was in 1951 that I first became associated with the Porsche car.

When motor sport restarted in 1945, with France running a motor race through the Bois du Boulogne in Paris in September of that year, overall control of the sport was a bit chaotic and diversified. Gradually some semblance of order was created and the threads of the international controlling body were picked up, both for car and for motorcycle racing. Germany was desperately trying to recover from the defeat and destruction it had suffered and two motor clubs were vying with each other to organize

The author in action with his Belgian friend Marcel Masuy on their Norton-Watsonian outfit at the Solituderennen in 1952 (author).

the sport. The International Federation told them they could not join the international scene, which meant that their members could not race outside Germany and other nations could not compete within Germany, until such time as they could become united within their own country. This internal power struggle dragged on for some time, finally settling itself with the formation of a single body to represent Germany on the international scene, but it was not until 1951 that international car races could be held in Germany.

The German sporting motorcycle scene was less complex and by 1950 they were allowed to organize semi-international motor cycle races, to which neighbouring countries could be invited. This meant, for example, that Belgian and Dutch riders could compete in Germany, but British riders could not. Swiss and French riders could cross into Germany to compete but Spanish and Italian riders could not. At the time I was living in Belgium, racing motorcycles and sidecars with a Belgian rider, so we were able to race in Germany before my English colleagues. It was due to this that I came across my first Porsche car in 1951, while at a race at Nuremburg, where the Nazi rallies had been held before the war, and where the War Crimes

The genial Hermann Böhm (left) with his passenger Karl Fuchs, when they were racing for the NSU factory in 1949. Between them is Gustav Germer, the NSU racing manager (NSU Archives).

Origins

tribunals were held immediately afterwards. The local club was organizing races on the roads around the old Nazi stadium, with the gigantic concrete tribune from which Hitler made his impassioned speeches as the main grandstand for spectators.

One of the top German sidecar riders was Hermann Böhm, who rode for the NSU factory, and we got to know him well. He was a very large man, weighing something like 220lb, and very genial, with a charming wife. When we met him at the Norisring, as the Nuremburg circuit was called, Noris being the original German name for Nürnburg, or Nuremburg as we English spell it, he proudly showed us his new car. It was a black Porsche 356 coupé, and alongside Böhm it looked tiny. He offered Marcel and me a ride. Being small, I climbed into the space behind the seats, while Hermann and Marcel occupied the front, and I must say I was impressed that such a large man could get into such a small car.

Those early Porsches had 1,300cc engines in which the crankshaft ran on roller bearings, so they were pretty noisy mechanically. Sitting sideways in the back, leaning against the rear bulkhead between the cockpit and the engine compartment, I could feel the rumblings of the roller bearings apart from hearing them. However, what was interesting was that as speed increased the noise diminished, for the noise from the engine was being wafted out the back and the streamlined shape generated very little wind noise. In fact, the way that little coupé cut through the air at 80mph was very impressive. I had never been in anything that sat so low on the ground, at least not since a Brooklands Riley of pre-war days, but that was virtually a sports/racing car. This totally enclosed, aerodynamic coupé was really impressive, and because it was so low it held the road like the proverbial leech, scuttling round corners with no drama whatsoever, there being little sensation of roll. Being so pleased with and proud of his new car, Hermann gave us a good demonstration, for at that time few people had new cars, let alone a new Porsche, a car from an entirely new manufacturer. That little black coupé made a lasting impression on me.

As I was heavily involved with motorcycle racing in Europe, cars did not come into my life very much, apart from large American Buicks and Chevrolets which we used to tow our trailer full of bikes. At the Earls Court Motor Show in 1951, two Porsche coupés were on show, brought over by Connaught Cars Ltd. To the motoring enthusiast, these smooth, streamlined coupés were impressive, as was the performance generated by a mere 44 brake horsepower from the 1,286-cc engine. Light weight, low drag and high gearing accounted for the way these coupés went. Before the Motor Show, the Editor of *Motor Sport* was taken out in one of them and was sufficiently impressed to write a half-page article on his brief run 'up the road and back'.

Two early Porsches seen in the Nurburgring paddock in the early 1950s. On the right is one of the very early aluminium competition coupés and on the left a split-windscreen production 356 (author).

As Connaught Cars Ltd became more and more involved in building racing cars, they passed the Porsche agency over to Colborne-Baber who had premises just down the road from them. At Earls Court the media was more excited about these Porsche cars being the first post-war German cars to appear in Great Britain, than about their motoring merit, but the more knowledgeable people who looked at them could see their true worth.

One of these people was W. H. (Bill) Aldington, the eldest of the three brothers who ran AFN Ltd and built Frazer Nash cars. Bill Aldington had come to know the German motor industry very well in the 1930s when he and his brothers were importing BMW cars and motorcycles, and he saw in the Porsche car just the sort of thing which their clientele could use. His brother, H. J., who was the real driving force behind AFN Ltd, was heavily involved with the Bristol car and his own Frazer Nash cars, principally because he could use the Bristol support for his fanatical interest in racing, but Bill Aldington was looking further ahead. It was no surprise therefore to find that AFN Ltd took over the Porsche agency before very long. Due to this, I became very involved with Porsche cars and a subsequent owner and member of the Porsche 'family'.

Chapter THREE

Indoctrination

Once AFN Ltd had got their Porsche agency under way, they naturally increased their sales staff and a very good friend of mine, Michael Burn, joined them as Porsche sales manager at their showrooms in Isleworth. Meanwhile I was still operating in Europe, having finished with motorcycle racing and taken on the role of 'roving race reporter' for the magazine *Motor Sport*. I was using a 1939 Lancia Aprilia saloon for my travels, a delightful little car of very advanced design that was great fun to drive. It's true that you could not see very much out of the tiny rear window in the sloping tail, but in those days there was not much worth seeing behind you so it did not matter. With all four wheels independently sprung and a good, rigid monocoque body/chassis unit, it handled remarkably well and could be cornered with complete abandon. With a cruising speed of 65mph, you could easily put 50 miles into the hour on a cross-country run.

After seven years of continuous motorcycle racing, it was not easy to withdraw completely from competitions, so when the occasion arose I entered the little Lancia Aprilia for minor events such as hill climbs. These had to be fitted into my travels, which meant arriving in the paddock, unloading my luggage, tools, spare parts and general travelling paraphernalia, doing the event, loading up and continuing on my way to my next reporting assignment. At one of these events, at Planfoy near St Etienne in Central France, I was competing with the Aprilia when I met a short, wiry little German driver, with quite thick spectacles: an eager and vital personality of enormous enthusiasm for motoring and motor racing. This was Richard von Frankenberg who raced a Porsche 1500 Super coupé. He knew me by sight

The author's Lancia Aprilia saloon in the paddock at a French hill climb, between a 1900 Alfa Romeo and a 203 Peugeot (author).

The start of the Planfoy hill climb was up the main cobbled street of the town. A 4½-litre Talbot Lago is seen on its way to start the climb (author).

Indoctrination

The bespectacled Richard von Frankenberg in the cockpit of a Porsche in Sweden in 1955 (author).

A Passion for Porsches

from my motorcycle racing days, and during practice he introduced himself to me. As he was on his own, and so was I, we spent most of the weekend together and he instilled Porsche philosophy into me, suggesting that a Porsche would be much more fun for me than my old Aprilia. I did not argue with him, it was just a question of finance.

During the weekend he took me for a run in his 1500 Super which was in effect a competition version, and as he was one of the leading exponents of Porsche driving in those days, it was most impressive. Those early Porsches, with no anti-roll bar for the front suspension, and with swing-axle rear suspension, were easily affected by the rearward weight distribution due to having the engine out behind the rear axle. They slid their rear wheels out in a corner very easily, in what is known as oversteer. Frankenburg's method of control was to provoke this tail slide sooner than the car wanted to do it naturally, and then neutralize it instantly by correcting the steering: before the car could react to this steering input, he would provoke it again into oversteer. The result was that the car 'wiggled' round the corner with the back-end virtually trembling on the brink of a total skid. It meant working away very fast on the steering and keeping a nice balance between losing and maintaining control, and it was very effective. However, if you got out of step you were in real trouble and the car could do a flick-roll on to its roof before you knew where you were. Frankenberg called this method of cornering a Porsche *'wischening'* or 'wiping' and it really was quite easy to do, as I was to find out later.

As I have mentioned, my friend Michael Burn was by now selling Porsche cars from AFN Ltd in Isleworth and was naturally well to the fore at the Earls Court Motor Show in London. One evening during the Show, we arranged to leave early and go down to Hampshire to our local motor club to attend a talk being given by Nancy Mitchell on her rallying experiences. Michael arranged to borrow the Show 'demonstrator' Porsche for this trip and when we met up on the AFN stand I had my chum Sandy Burnett with me while Michael had arranged to take Tom Lush from the Allard stand with him. Remarkably, all four of us squeezed into the car, Tom and Sandy being determined to do so as they had never been in a Porsche. Michael and Tom sat in the front, both being well over 6 foot tall, and somehow Sandy and I folded ourselves up into the space behind the seats. My lasting impression of that ride down to Eversley in the dark was hearing Tom say quietly, 'I didn't realize that London buses ran on Michelin Heavy Duty tyres'. Every time we stopped in the London traffic we seemed to be beside a bus, and all Tom could see when he looked sideways out of the Porsche was the wording on the tyres of the buses, level with his eyes. It made us conscious of just how low the Porsche 356 coupé was.

Indoctrination

By now I was starting negotiations to acquire a Porsche to replace the Lancia Aprilia, as Richard von Frankenberg had suggested back in the summer. Early in February 1955, Michael asked if I would like to join him on a sales promotion and customer relations trip on behalf of AFN Ltd to the West of England. It was going to involve three days of motoring around Dorset and Devon and the weather was spring-like, so I wasted no time in joining him. We shared the driving of the AFN Ltd 'demonstrator' 356 coupé. At one point, while he went to see various agents and dealers, he left me at the home of an enthusiastic Porsche owner in Bovey Tracey. This was Dr Harrison who was running a Porsche 1500 Super. During the day, he kindly let me drive his car for a 50-mile dice over Dartmoor and the surrounding countryside. As I have said, the weather was spring-like and quite unlike a normal February, so it was sheer joy to wind up the little blue coupé on the deserted roads: there were no speed restrictions in those days. The Super engine had a crankshaft running on roller bearings, apart from bigger carburettors and ports and a higher compression ratio, so that it gave 70bhp against the normal engine's 55bhp and revved freely to 5,500rpm.

Michael Burn adjusts the radio aerial on the AFN Porsche 'demonstrator' in the early spring sunshine at Sidmouth, during the author's trip to the West Country in 1955 (author).

A Passion for Porsches

By using the gearbox you could really keep it on the boil. The horsepower figures were those quoted by the Porsche factory. Apart from the fact that they were DIN figures, it was always reckoned that they were deliberately well under the actual figures as German insurance was based on horsepower ratings supplied by the manufacturers. By this time I did not need much indoctrination about Porsche cars, but any chinks that remained were ably filled in by Dr Harrison.

Back in the white 'demonstrator', we returned to another appointment in Dorset and finally set off for home in the dark. We had had our three days of glorious weather and rain was spreading from the east, so Michael elected to drive back as my night-time vision is very poor. Michael was one of those fortunate people who did not need spectacles to see properly and he had fantastic night-vision. This rare attribute is something which you are born with, and if you haven't got it there is no point in worrying about it. I did quite a lot of motoring with Michael Burn in those days and I used to doubt this night-driving ability. I would often quiz him on it, getting him to tell me what he could see and read ahead as soon as possible, and I found it was seconds before I could see the same things. The clarity of his vision at night in the light of headlamps never ceased to amaze me.

We left the West Country on a Thursday evening, and as it was the first Thursday in the month this meant that the regular Vintage Sports Car Club meeting was being held at the Phoenix pub in Hartley Wintney on the A30 road. This was long before motorways were heard of in England, but equally it was long before traffic density became impossible. Michael wound the little Porsche up well and truly, and we did the last 65 miles in 56 minutes, sitting in virtual silence and extreme comfort and security. This was in the days when sports cars were still pretty rorty and spartan, and family saloons were struggling to attain 76mph as a maximum. By the time I got home I was totally sold on Porsches and was looking forward to acquiring a 1,500-cc 356A, the latest version, with an anti-roll bar fitted to the front suspension and fully reclining seats made by the Reutter firm next door to the Porsche factory in the Zuffenhausen suburb of Stuttgart.

Chapter FOUR

Joining the family

With the assistance of H. J. (Aldy) Aldington of AFN Ltd and Richard von Frankenburg, I was able to pick up a brand new 356A from the factory. As I was planning some fairly extensive European motoring in it, I settled for the normal 1,500-cc engine, the resultant model being known at the factory as the *'Damen'* or *'Lady'*. Once again I had the opportunity to experience *'wischening'* as practised by von Frankenberg, as he picked me up from Stuttgart airport and took me to Zuffenhausen, where my Adriatic blue coupé was awaiting me. When you got those early Porsches really cornering near the limit, the whole engine/gearbox unit was going through some very peculiar motions as the rear of the car went up and down and the swing axles travelled through the arcs of their length. Without warning the gear lever would suddenly flap violently sideways and that, according to Richard, meant that you were about on the limit of the cornering power. After warning me to keep my knees well over to the side of the car, he demonstrated what he was saying as we went through the suburbs of Stuttgart. If you had your knees over towards the centre of the car, you could receive a really nasty clout from the gear lever knob, so before indulging in any violent cornering it was as well to make sure your passenger's knees were well to one side, especially if they were feminine knees.

In those days of almost individual sales, when customers were known by their Christian names, a new car was delivered to the factory gates with a full tank of petrol, handbooks and paperwork, and some words of advice from a member of the sales staff. As a writer I was looked after by the press department, a very important and active part of the Porsche organization,

The author's pristine and new 356A Porsche parked in a friendly manner alongside a Belgian-owned Speedster seen in a French town in 1955. The spot-lamps on the bumper were mounted askew for looking across mountain hairpin bends; the flame-thrower in the middle for seeing into the far distance.

and von Frankenberg, who was editor of the house magazine *Christophorous* as well as being a factory racing driver, did the official handing over of my car. He also presented me with a Porsche umbrella, which was in the latest German style and folded up into a small tubular holder. It was a grey umbrella with the name Porsche in red all round the edge, but it was not the normal umbrella shape when erected. This latest German fashion decreed a very shallow curvature to the canopy, like an inverted saucer rather than an inverted bowl. When Richard gave it to me, he chuckled and said, 'and when you open it, you will find it is low and streamlined, like a Porsche.'

My blue coupé had a sliding panel in the roof, the new longer lifting handle on the front lid, extra rubbing strips along the sides and the latest fully reclining seats, a Blaupunkt push-button radio, the front anti-roll bar and the model name 'Continental', proclaimed by means of a metal name plate on each side. The name was short-lived as Lincoln were using it, for a very different sort of car, so the model soon reverted to the simple Porsche 1500 Normal. The driver's manual supplied with the car put you in the right frame of mind at once, for on page 1 it read, 'Judging you by the car you own, you rank among the class of discriminating motorists' and it ended up with,

Joining the family

'We wish you many thousands of miles of pleasure with your Porsche.' From the start, your ego was boosted and you knew that Dr Ing hc F. Porsche KG of Stuttgart-Zuffenhausen were building cars that were meant to be driven for fun, not merely as utility appliances. Another owners' welcoming publication mentioned that the Porsche family of owners was not very large but very closely knit, and that Porsche drivers always gave a flash of the headlights as a form of greeting to other Porsche owners. I had not gone far in my new acquisition before I saw another Porsche, and sure enough the lights flashed momentarily and I replied with the little lever on the steering column, feeling immensely pleased with myself. I was now a member of the Porsche family.

This headlamp flashing between Porsche owners was universal all over Europe and was always a source of pleasure, but it died out eventually when the Westfalia police took to using Porsche Speedsters and Cabriolets as patrol cars. They did not find it amusing to see a Porsche *'wischening'* towards

A Porsche Speedster of 1955 which the author borrowed from the factory. It was a truly open two-seater with a collapsible top, but defeated the good aerodynamics of the normal 356 models (author).

A Passion for Porsches

The type of Porsche you did not flash your headlamps at. The Austrian police also used Porsche Speedsters as patrol cars, fitted with radio telephones. To avoid being bracketed with the German Polizei, the Austrian police are called Gendarmerie.

them and giving a flash of the headlights in mid-corner! Also, it became embarassing when you were breaking the speed limit or doing a dodgy bit of overtaking, to see a Porsche coming the other way and to find it was a police car, after you had flashed your lights and given a cheery wave.

Driving the little 'beetle' Porsche was a passport to friendship anywhere in Europe. Conversation would start with 'Is that your blue Porsche over there?' in almost any language. I struck up friendships with Porsche owners from Sweden to Portugal, and from the north of England to Sicily. You could say that Porsche owners were a 'race apart' in those days; perhaps they were, but there is no doubt that they all loved motoring and loved driving their Porsches. There was also a tremendous feeling of pride in being in a Porsche when you went to race meetings or rallies, for the factory was very active in the more serious and tough events like the 1,000 kilometres of Nurburgring, the Le Mans 24 Hour race, the Liège-Rome-Liège rally, the Alpine rally and so on. Even as the mere driver of a *'Damen'*, you felt part of this growing family and got great satisfaction out of watching more affluent and skilful people demonstrating Porsche prowess in competition.

The Porsche press and public relations department followed up the sales

Relative to the normal 356 coupés, the Speedster was spartan, with less trim in the cockpit, smaller and lighter seats and so on, and weighed quite a bit less than the normal car (author).

The cockpit of the Cabriolet cars used by the Austrian police was equipped with a radio telephone. The two-spoke steering wheel had grown a full-circle horn-ring by this time (author).

A Passion for Porsches

To promote Porsche feeling in the home, the factory had a dinner service made in 1960 depicting various 356 series scenes. It was all part of spreading the gospel according to Dr Porsche.

The rather subtle enamelled badge given to early Porsche owners who covered 100,000 kilometres in their 356 models without the lower end of the engine needing attention.

Joining the family

side of the firm with a constant flow of what people now call Porsche Memorabilia, but at the time they were merely adjuncts to being a Porsche owner. Some of these things, like silk scarves and purses, were to keep the owner's wife or girl friend Porsche-minded, other domestic items such as plates with Porsche pictures on them kept the whole family Porsche-orientated, and some were for the pure satisfaction of the driver. One such was a neat little badge for the front of the car which depicted a stretch of Autobahn disappearing into the distance with the name PORSCHE across it, while at the top it simply read 100,000km. This badge was given to you if you completed 100,000 kilometres in your car without having anything done to the bottom end of the engine. The nice thing about it was that if you were not in the Porsche family, you had no idea what the badge represented.

All these small things made you very aware that the factory was not just interested in its customers, but in motoring, in exactly the same way as the customers were interested. All the VIPs in the factory drove Porsches in the normal course of events, except Karl Rabe of the design department, who insisted on always driving about in a Volkswagen. When you were in

Even in conditions like this, the 356A would fire up instantly and drive off with little fuss, leaving front-engined, rear-drive cars and those with automatic transmission in a helpless situation.

A Passion for Porsches

Zuffenhausen you would see Dr Ferry Porsche arriving in a Porsche, usually the latest production model, and sometimes an experimental model. At race meetings the factory drivers and the engineers would arrive in Porsches, as well they might, for apart from putting in useful test-miles on experimental cars and parts, they were well aware that a Porsche was one of the best ways of getting about Europe.

Over the next few years I was to spend quite a lot of time with Richard von Frankenberg, and he taught me a great deal about Porsche cars and Porsche driving and introduced me into a close-knit family of Porsche owners and their own special mythology. While I was staying with Richard one winter, we went out to visit some friends, both in our Porsches, and during the evening there was a heavy fall of snow. There were some other friends at the gathering, one in a 220A Mercedes-Benz and another in an Opel, and when it was time to leave Richard and I got into our Porsches and just drove off. The others sat there spinning their wheels in the snow and had to be helped away, the Mercedes-Benz owner being in real trouble because his car had automatic transmission and an automatic choke. With a cold engine and no clutch he had a terrible time. The little Porsches with their engine weight over the rear axle and no transmission line to 'wind-up' were the easiest things to drive on snow and ice, for they had remarkable traction. Later on, there was much 'ribbing' of our unfortunate friends with their conventional cars.

One night I was motoring in my own Porsche on the Autobahn towards

At one time my friends thought I was becoming obsessed with German automotive engineering and suggested that my house was beginning to look like the German embassy! Admittedly I had an R51 BMW motorcycle and a 1936 Mercedes-Benz as well as the Porsche 356A (author).

Joining the family

Richard von Frankenberg rounding the south curve at the AVUS track in Berlin in 'Mickey Mouse', ahead of an East German EMW driven by Edgar Barth, who later joined the Porsche factory.

A Passion for Porsches

Stuttgart, and as was normal I was flat out. The Porsche 356 was nicely over-geared so that you could not burst the engine even if you drove it flat out from Berlin to Munich. I could see the headlights of another Porsche behind me and we ran in close company for mile after mile. I was heading for von Frankenberg's house, where I had arranged to stay for a day or two, and had no idea it was him following me, at least not until I turned off the Autobahn on to the back roads leading to where he lived. When we arrived home he explained how he knew it was me ahead of him, even though he could not recognize me in the dark and did not know my registration number. He read his rev-counter and knew that the Porsche in front was a *'Damen'* and was going flat out. When he first came up behind me his rev-counter told him I was travelling at 4,200rpm and he felt that if it had been a 1500 Super I would have been doing more like 4,800rpm on that particular stretch of Autobahn. On one long hill the rpm dropped back to 3,800 and he was then certain it was a *'Damen'*, for a Super would have held 4,000. On another incline he saw a puff of smoke from my exhaust as I changed into third gear that much sooner than he did; pulling 5,000rpm up that particular incline in third gear assured him that it was a normal 1,500cc car, for a Super would have pulled 5,500rpm easily. 'Ah!' he said, 'I knew then that this must be Denis ahead of me, heading for the house of Frankenberg.' In those days there were not many Porsches on Stuttgart registration plates and anyway he knew all the owners within 50 miles of the Porsche factory.

Sadly Richard von Frankenberg was killed in a stupid road accident, after risking his life racing Porsches for many years and surviving some pretty horrific racing accidents. One in particular was a 'near thing', when he went over the top of the steep banking on the AVUS track in Berlin. He was racing an experimental Porsche Spyder that belonged to the factory. This was much shorter in the wheelbase than the normal racing/sports car and he always referred to it as 'Mickey Mouse'. It was pretty twitchy in the dry and a real handful in the wet, but Richard knew no fear and was hurtling round the lip of the banking when it spun for no apparent reason and projected him over the top. Miraculously he escaped unhurt and lived to race another day. Some years after he had retired from racing, he was driving home on a winter's night. As he peeled off the Autobahn on to the semi-circular exit road, the car in front of him spun round on sheet ice, turned over and caught fire. Richard's Porsche slid helplessly into the burning wreck and he died.

Chapter FIVE

Friends

As I mentioned in the previous chapter, the 'beetle' Porsche was an instant passport to conversation in any language. One of my earliest experiences of this was at the Pau Grand Prix in 1955, when an American photographer murmered to me, 'That your Porsche? I've got one.' This was Jesse Alexander, a quiet, gentle, man, who was photographing and reporting on European races for various American magazines and living in Switzerland with his wife and four daughters. He had travelled to Pau from Geneva on more or less the same route as I had taken, across the south of France, through Nimes, Montpelier, Narbonne and Carcassonne, and we compared notes on our journeys. Jesse's feelings on the Porsche were summed up by his brief phrase, 'great little cars, aren't they.' We found we had cruised at the same speeds on the same roads and that our idea of Porsche motoring was identical. 'Did you hold 90mph along that stretch by the canal?' 'Yes'; 'and reach 4,600 in top on that long stretch through the poplar trees?'; 'Exactly'. It was fascinating: we could have been in the same car. '. . . and averaged 32mpg . . .'; 'Yes, precisely': happy Porsche owners preening themselves in mutual admiration and basking in the satisfaction afforded by Dr Porsche!

About a month later I met Jesse again, in Brescia from where the famous Mille Miglia race started, and he introduced me to a German Porsche owner he had met: Wolfgang Graf Berghe von Trips, the young nobleman from near Cologne who was racing a 1500 Super in the Mille Miglia. Later I was to become great friends with von Trips and to enjoy a lot of motoring with him, as is recounted in another chapter. When I had a drink with Jesse and his wife

Jesse Alexander's Porsche 356B on Swiss number plates is seen in the Italian mountains south of Bologna at Mille Miglia time.

Wolfgang von Trips' Porsche 356 and the author's car outside the family castle at Hörrem near Cologne in 1955. Note that von Trips had dispensed with hub caps and bumper trim, whereas the author had not yet started serious competitions with his car.

Friends

after the race, they were full of enthusiasm for von Trips, for not only was he a charming young man but his enthusiasm for racing and motoring and the Porsche way of life was enormous and infectious. He was also a very good driver and progressed into the factory Mercedes-Benz and Ferrari racing teams, as well as the Porsche factory team. In that 1955 Mille Miglia his accelerator cable had broken, so he wired the two carburettors on to full throttle and completed the 1,000 miles by using the ignition switch to cut the engine in and out as required. He viewed the whole affair as a riot of fun and roared with laughter as he recounted some of the hair-raising situations his Porsche got into during that drive. He finished second in his class, behind Richard von Frankenberg. His spirit and enthusiasm was totally irrepressible and he exuded pleasure wherever he went and in whatever he did. On occasions I would stay with him at his family home at Hörrem, not too far from the Nurburgring, and we would travel there in convoy in our Porsches, his silver car looking very beaten up and well worn externally as he was more interested in the way it went than in how it looked.

The family home was literally a castle and at one time had a moat round it and a drawbridge. His mother and father were from aristocratic stock and lived there in a sort of quiet, faded elegance. Even though the moat and the drawbridge were no longer to be seen, once inside the von Trips home there was a comfortable feeling that the drawbridge was up and the moat was full and you were safe from the outside world. His parents did not approve of Wolfgang racing, and like so many young people from such families he started racing under an assumed name so that his parents would not know, but then made the fateful mistake of winning. He won a small event at the Nurburgring and his photo appeared in a local newspaper under his assumed name, but his father saw it and recognized him, so there were big explanations demanded. When it was obvious that his passion for racing was unquenchable, his parents relented and gave approval, but as so often happens, they regretted it the day he was killed in the Italian Grand Prix at Monza in 1961.

My friendship with Jesse Alexander and our love of Porsches went on for many years and is still as strong as ever, even though he has long since returned to the United States and California. I still see him when I visit Los Angeles for the Long Beach Grand Prix each year and we still have that same feeling and admiration for Dr Porsche and his factory, even though we no longer use Porsche cars. While in Switzerland Jesse had a house built in the mountains at Hohfluh, on the opposite side of the Meiringen valley to the Matterhorn, and from his lounge window you had a magnificent view of that famous mountain. It was no ordinary house, for it was designed by Frank Lloyd Wright, who was noted for producing houses in much the same

The house designed by Frank Lloyd Wright and built by the Swiss for Jesse Alexander in the mountains at Hohfluh, looking across the valley to the Matterhorn.

way as Picasso produced paintings, and it was executed by a Swiss architect and a local firm. Ernst, the architect, became a close friend of the family, so close in fact that he eventually bought Jesse's original Porsche 356A. When I last saw Ernst, many years ago now, he had done a phenomenal mileage in the car. Jesse had done something like 100,000 miles in it before he sold it and the engine had never been taken apart. It had not led a sheltered life by any means, but it had never been used in competition.

Friends

Although Jesse loved motor racing and all its facets he had no urge to take part, unlike myself and various other friends who could not resist some form of competition, so that our cars got abused in the heat and excitement of racing.

One such friend was Steve Wilder, another American in Europe, this time an ex-GI who somehow had forgotten to go home. He had been based in England with the American army and so enjoyed the motor sporting club life that he stayed on when he was demobbed and got himself a 1500 Super Porsche, very much like Wolfgang von Trips' car, outwardly a bit scruffy but right on the button as regards performance. Steve was a good practical fellow who could whip a Porsche engine out by the roadside and fix it if need be, so we got on well together. I took him with me on a rapid trip to Bari, well down the Adriatic coast of Italy. It was in 1956 and we had been at Silverstone for the weekend. We left the following Tuesday evening and drove virtually non-stop to arrive at Bari on Friday.

We had one stop, however, though not from our choosing. In those days there were no Autostrade down the Adriatic coast and the roads were pretty rough, but in the Porsche we just hammered on regardless. We were pounding along not far from Bari when the car suddenly slewed across the road and made an awful noise, and I fought it to a stop by the roadside. We got out to see what had happened and found the right rear wheel tucked up under the body and that corner scraping on the ground. Our first thoughts were that the rear axle tube had broken, but it turned out to be nothing more serious than the wheel breaking off around the fixing bolt holes. It had obviously been cracked for some time by the look of it, no doubt brought on by hard *'wischening'* on rough roads. Luckily, no damage was done apart from a slight tweak to the bodywork, so we fitted the spare wheel and completed our journey.

That trip took in the race at Bari, the following weekend at Le Mans for the 24 Hour Race, followed by the German Grand Prix at the Nurburgring, by which time my Porsche was suffering from a worn-out front gearbox mounting. In the Nurburgring paddock we dropped the engine and gearbox out and renewed the rubber mounting, and for that sort of job 'in the field' Steve was an ace.

My own particular urge to keep doing some sort of motoring competition, no matter how small, saw me competing in sprints and hill climbs and the 750 Motor Club's 6 Hour Relay Race, and through these activities I made many more Porsche friends. One particularly good one was Jack Burke, who had a 1500-cc Carrera Porsche with which he was extremely generous, letting both Steve and me borrow it for events, as well as competing with it himself. Jack drove hard and fast on the road and that Carrera was well used. He rang me

Jack Burke and his daughter Pat, pose for the author's camera in front of their Carrera in the square at Mons, on the way to the Bruxelles Expo in 1958.

Friends

one day to say he had had a minor accident with it, clobbering a parked car. I went down to his home near Southampton to see what the damage was and it turned out to be very extensive, even though there was little to show for it. The bumper on the front of the 356 series cars was mounted on 'horns' that bolted to the chassis box that formed the front of the car, and if you were unlucky and hit something with only one of the mountings it could lozenge the whole chassis box. The indication of this was a kink in the body panel in front of the windscreen on the opposite side to that which had been struck. Jack had rammed the parked car with his left front corner and, sure enough, there was the dreaded kink by the right-hand screen pillar. This meant having the whole front of the car cut off and a new chassis box welded on. My German Porsche friends had warned me about this and recommended hitting things fair and square with both bumper mounts, if you had any choice. Far better, however, was to discard the front bumper altogether and risk damaging the doubleskinned nose, which was far cheaper to repair after a minor shunt. Once I started using my 356A seriously for competitions, I dispensed with both bumpers and fitted the rubber and aluminium rubbing strip directly to the bodywork, which looked neat and was very effective.

Another friend that accrued through the Porsche family was the Scottish racing enthusiast Ian Scott-Watson, who ran a 1600 Super. Ian's friendship opened up another one that had far-reaching results. While Steve Wilder and I were competing in small club events, the main opposition came from Triumph TR2 sports cars. Except for the really hot ones, they were fair game. Steve's Porsche had a tweaked-up 1500 Super engine in it and he was consistently faster than me, whether up a hill or on a single sprint lap of Brands Hatch. We were able to evaluate Porsche performances pretty accurately, and knew how they matched up to the TR Triumphs depending on their state of tune. While Steve could just hang on to the better TR2, he could never beat them and he was always fascinated to read the results of Scottish club events in *Autosport*, for the TR element north of the border was always getting beaten by a 1600S Porsche driven by a Mr J. Clark. We knew nothing about this J. Clark, and reckoned that either the TR opposition wasn't very good or he was a very fast driver. Steve followed the club world closely and soon established that the hot Scottish TR2s were every bit the equal of those down south, so this J. Clark interested us. When Ian Scott-Watson said that he was going to join the 1958 Six Hours Relay Race Porsche team with his 1600 Super, and that Jim Clark would be journeying south to Silverstone with him to drive it, we pricked up our ears. In a letter to me before the event, Ian said 'Jimmy is a very good driver.' Both Steve and I pictured a large rugged Scot with great hairy knees below his kilt, probably

A Passion for Porsches

Jimmy Clark, the farmer from Duns in Scotland, who raced a Porsche 1600S in his early competition days. Before his untimely death at Hockenheim in Germany, he not only became World Champion but the 'best' in the eyes of many people.

Friends

smoking a pipe, and with all the appearance of having been hewn from a block of granite. Steve said, 'Gee, he must be a rugged character to keep beating the TR brigade. I drive like hell and can just about hang on to them.'

Imagine our surprise when we got to Silverstone and Ian introduced a slight, almost demure, young man who looked as if he should still have been wearing a school cap, and said, 'This is Jimmy Clark.' Steve and I wandered off looking puzzled, asking each other, 'Is that really the Jim Clark we've been reading about?' Once practice started there was no question. He was so fast it was almost embarrassing, and he had never been near Silverstone before. Our calculations and estimations of lap times, taking into account car performance and driver ability, were hopelessly out. After practice I kept meeting marshals who had been out on the circuit, who said 'Who is driving that white Porsche in your team? He's fantastic.' It was J. Clark from Scotland who later became World Champion and acknowledged number one the world over. Jack Burke let him have a go in his Carrera. His lap times were incredible for a 1500-cc car and he really enjoyed the extra power of the 4-camshaft engine. Eventually he spun it and put a slight dent in the tail, returning full of apologies for his bad behaviour, but Jack was not worried: he was still off the ground with excitement at seeing his car being driven so fast.

Another Porsche fanatic I got to know through competitions was Welshman Tommy Pascoe, who was running a yellow Speedster fitted with a hard top in all the club events in southern England. Tommy was already fairly advanced in years even then, but it did not deter him from thrashing his Porsche well and truly. The miles it has done must be astronomical and today it is owned by his son, who still gives it an airing occasionally, for old times' sake.

In Europe many of the Porsche friends I made moved up into the international racing world, people such as Claude Storez, Jean Behra, Auguste Vieullet and Robert Buchet, and I got to know them through my journalistic reporting as well as through Porsche ownership.

In 1957 I met up with a bunch of Californian 'hot-rodders', all members of the original Californian Road Runners, who came to Europe to take part in the Mille Miglia with a Chrysler V8-powered hot-rod built by Akton Miller, an arch-priest of 'tune' in Los Angeles. Jesse Alexander was their link-man in Europe so naturally we all spent a lot of time together. 'Uncle Ak', as he was called, had Doug Harrison as his passenger and Peter Coltrin as his general 'go-fer' and helper. Pete had not long left the US Army and was known as the 'Lootenant'. Apart from his interest in the trip, he contributed the tow-car for the outfit, or to be more precise, his mother did. This was an Oldsmobile

'Uncle' Ak Miller at his Californian works with a jet-propelled record car he built for a customer in 1961. Today, Ak Miller is very involved with turbo-charging, from Volkswagen Golf diesel pick-ups to 7-litre Chevrolet 'hot-rods'.

coupé to which a tow-bar had been added, and Ak had lifted out mother's standard V8 engine and dropped in one of his own rather special V8 units, basically an Oldsmobile, but with various go-faster goodies on it. The Chrysler-powered sports car was on a trailer behind Mrs Coltrin's coupé and Jesse and I did not take much notice of the entourage, other than their entry

Friends

in the Mille Miglia. Unfortunately, Ak and Doug did not get far in the race as they had brake trouble, but they stayed on in Europe after the event and Pete stayed with them. Apart from visiting various places, they also went to some European Grand Prix races and eventually we all met up at Jesse's house at Hohfluh, which Ak insisted on calling 'Hoflush', adding afterwards, 'on the Rhine', as he was sure that the River Rhine covered the whole of Europe.

Their return trip was from Cherbourg and since Jesse and I were heading for a race at Rouen at the time of departure, we arranged to travel in convoy and show them the way. Condescendingly Jesse and I agreed that we were not

Porsche drivers. The author obviously concentrating on something else from the Nurburgring pits in 1959, with Jesse Alexander on the left and Peter Coltrin on the right. The two Californians drove 356B coupés.

A Passion for Porsches

in a hurry, so we did not mind the Oldsmobile and trailer keeping station behind us.

My first inkling of embarrassment was after breakfast when Ak went out to start up the Oldsmobile and warm it up, for I had not even looked at it at this point. It had the smoothest and sweetest running V8 engine I had ever heard. I had become used to American V8 engines in things like Allards and Cunninghams, but this was something else and Ak was very proud of it, for it was a typical Miller-prepared overhead-valve V8. That journey to Rouen was a terrible embarrassment to Jesse and me, for on the long straights across France that great bulbous Oldsmobile coupé with the trailer and racing car on the back sat behind us no matter what we did. We both rowed our little Porsches along as hard as we could, cruising continually at 85 mph, and the Miller entourage just sat there in our mirrors. What was worse, Ak, Doug and Pete were sitting abreast on the bench seat smoking cigars, while Ak drove with one hand on the wheel and his elbow on the window ledge in typical USA style. Meantime, both Jesse and I were driving our Porsches as if we

Everyone was keen to race the Porsche 550 Spyders, and Stirling Moss is seen here with the one he used to win the 1,500-cc race at Lisbon in 1955. Two similar cars driven by Portuguese drivers were second and third (author).

Peter Coltrin with his immaculate black 356B photographed 'round the back' of the Porsche service department in Zuffenhausen. Pete's obsession for an immaculate car led to disaster.

were competing in a race. When we stopped, AK removed his cigar and asked, 'Your little cars going OK?' That Oldsmobile coupé had been timed at Bonneville at something like 141mph using one of 'uncle Ak's' special V8 engines, but I don't think Pete's mother knew about that.

Two years later Peter Coltrin returned to Europe to live in Modena, where he married an Italian girl. He bought a 356B Porsche and joined the family, and over the years I did a great deal of Porsche motoring with him. Ak and Doug never returned to Europe, for Ak was a true-blue Californian hot-rodder and Doug went off to Mexico, but the 'Lootenant' had been bitten by the European racing bug and the Italian way of life, which he enjoyed to the full until he died quite suddenly early in 1982.

Chapter SIX

The Carrera

Very early on the Porsche factory committed itself to a programme of rallying and racing, encouraged by their early customers, and it was not long before they developed the basic Volkswagen engine to its ultimate limit as far as power was concerned. It continued for many years as a touring production engine, becoming more refined and efficient as the years went by, but for racing something new was needed. During the development of the push-rod engine one of the young designers, named Ernst Fuhrmann, produced a new camshaft and cam design that was a great success. When Ferry Porsche and Karl Rabe decided they needed a replacement engine for their racing work, Fuhrmann was given the brief. Both Ferry Porsche and Rabe spent a lot of time with Fuhrmann around his drawing board, in discussion and planning for the new engine during the early design days.

This new engine was design project number 547 and it had to fit in the same space as the existing engine, yet produce nearly twice the horsepower. Dr Fuhrmann laid out an air-cooled flat-4-cylinder engine, like the Volkswagen-based engines, but with inclined overhead valves in a new cylinder head design incorporating two overhead camshafts, so that the complete engine actually had four camshafts, 'overhead' relative to the valves and combustion chambers, but actually on each side of the horizontally opposed cylinder layout. These camshafts were driven by a train of bevel gears and shafts from the crankshaft and the engine was capable of very high rpm for the time. It was invariably known as the '4-cam engine' to distinguish it from the pushrod overhead-valve engines, and started life as a 1,500-cc unit.

This new engine first appeared in much secrecy for practice for a race at

The Carrera

the Nurburgring in 1953, mounted in a car that looked like a normal pushrod Spyder, except that the exhaust note was very different. Nobody was able to look under the engine cover and von Hanstein and Hans Herrmann drove it for a few laps before it was whisked away and covered over. Although the Porsche people tried to give the impression that it was just a normal racing Spyder, those who heard it in action knew differently, but nothing was revealed officially.

When it was announced the following year, it appeared in the new Type 550 Spyder sports/racing car and competed in the 1,000-mile Mille Miglia

A Carrera engine complete, standing on its ear. To appreciate it fully, turn the book through 90-degrees clockwise. Note the two camshaft boxes each side and the large cooling fan and ducting for the air-cooled cylinders and heads.

The name Carrera was to continue through the years of Porsche, a name synonymous with competition and seen here on a 2.7-litre 911 model.

road race in Italy, driven by Hans Herrmann and Herbert Linge. In spite of some minor troubles they finished sixth overall and won the 1,500-cc sports class. At the end of that season two 550 Spyders with the Type 547/1 4-cam engine were entered for the very fast Carrera Panamericana Mexico event, an event that ran the length of Mexico in daily stages and was known generally as the Mexican Road Race The word *'carrera'* is Spanish for 'race' and in Latin countries the event was merely called the *'Carrera'*. Once again Hans Herrmann was the factory driver and he finished a magnificent third overall behind two much larger-engined sports cars. Behind him in fourth place was another 550 Spyder using the new engine, driven by Jaroslav Juhan from Guatemala, his car also being entered by the factory. Naturally they were first and second in the 1,500-cc sports car class and the team returned to Germany highly delighted with their new racing engine, now that it was over its teething troubles.

The following year the 550 Spyder with the 4-cam engine was on sale to the sporting public, essentially for racing purposes, and in recognition of its Mexican success the engine adopted the name Carrera. Subsequently the engine was put into full scale production and made available in the 356 coupé

The Carrera

and Speedster models, and though the exact description was the 356A/1500GS with 547/1 engine, the model took on the name Carrera. Ever since that time the name Carrera has been synonymous with Porsche high-performance road-cars suitable for competition use. The 356A developed into the 1600-cc Carrera and finally into the 2-litre Carrera. Although the origin of the name was the Fuhrmann 4-cam engine, it was assigned to subsequent engines not designed by him. With the advent of the 911 Porsche series, the name Carrera was handed on and used on the various competition versions of that model, while today it is used on the special competition version of the 924.

In my formative Porsche years, the name Carrera was a new one to add to the vocabulary. It was synonymous with performance and came to be used as a by-word for hot Porsches, more than just an engine name. In fact, it passed into the motoring language so completely that there was no need to talk of Porsche Carrera, simply to say 'Carrera' was enough. Porsche had laid claim to the name by an undisputed performance in the Mexican Road Race and no-one had the temerity to try to usurp it. I wonder often whether the drivers of today's Carreras are aware of the origins of the name.

My first opportunity to drive a Porsche Carrera came quite by chance. Michael Burn needed someone to go with him to Gloucestershire to tow in

The author in his TT Replica Frazer Nash is seen leading a similar car at Gransden Lodge. This was shortly before he broke the engine and had to be towed home at higher speeds than those he had achieved in the race! (Louis Klemantaski).

The AFN Ltd saloon DKW that took Michael Burn and the author to Gloucestershire looking for a Carrera abandoned on a garage forecourt. The Carrera in question is on the right with Michael Burn investigating the engine compartment at the back.

Michael Burn investigating the engine of the abandoned Porsche Carrera. When the trouble was found to be merely incorrect setting of the petrol taps, the author was able to experience his first drive in a Carrera (author).

The Carrera

the AFN 'demonstrator' Carrera which had broken down, or so we were told. AFN had lent the car to Jon Pertwee, the actor, for a trip to the BBC Bristol studios, and he had phoned them to say it had died on him at Pennsylvania, just outside Bath. As he was short of time he had abandoned it on the forecourt of a garage and gone on by taxi. Michael picked me up in a DKW saloon and we headed west, first looking for the village of Pennsylvania, of which we had never heard, and then for a green Carrera abandoned on a garage forecourt. The idea was to hitch a rope to it and for me to be towed back to London in it, Michael and I having been involved in many towing escapades together in our formative motoring years, including some classic trips with our mutual friend Holland Birkett. It is worth deviating a bit from Porsche activity to recount two particular tow jobs I did just after the war when racing restarted.

Holland Birkett was a great Bugatti enthusiast and he had a 5-litre Type 46 straight-8 Bugatti fitted with an open pick-up body, weighing very little compared to the original cabriolet body for which the car had been built. Consequently, its performance was pretty exciting and it was used as an all purpose vehicle, including some club racing. We had all been to the first Gransden Lodge airfield meeting, in which Holly raced the Bugatti, I raced my TT Replica Frazer Nash and another friend raced his Velocette motorcycle. In my race I ran all my big ends and Holly agreed to tow me back to Hampshire behind the Bugatti. Our motorcycle friend had to return to London so we agreed to take his Velocette back home with us, and various friends came along as the pick-up body could easily carry the motorcycle and half a dozen people.

Now my Frazer Nash could do about 75mph, with just on 80mph down an incline with the screen folded flat, so imagine my horror when we set off across the wastes of Cambridgeshire and my speedometer showed 85mph. The 5-litre Bugatti was good for well over 90mph but Birkett thought he would take it easy as he had a full load on board and the Nash on tow on a rope. I was helpless since all I could see was the high tail board of the Bugatti and in those days we had no such things as brake lights. By the time we got home the Frazer Nash brakes were nearly red hot and I was a gibbering wreck. I had never travelled so fast nor accelerated so rapidly under my own power, let alone on the end of a tow rope.

On another occasion about this time, we were at the Brighton Speed Trials and a friend asked if we could tow his 1½-litre ERA racing car home for him, as he had to go off somewhere else. This time Holly Birkett was in his 3-litre Bugatti, another rapid 8-cylinder with a light four-seater body. Somehow I had got the reputation for being an ace on the end of a tow rope, so I was put in the ERA and Michael and Holly and the others got in the Bugatti. They were happy carefree days, when we towed anything and everything on a slack rope. Nobody bothered about insurance, trailer boards, winkers, brake lights, mudguards or any other legalities: we just tied on a rope and off we went. We were cruising along very nicely at about 70–75mph and I was in my element in a single-seater racing car on the public highway, even if the engine wasn't running. As we breasted a rise a small saloon car turned across the road in front of the Bugatti and the next few moments were incredibly busy. I never really saw what the Bugatti did, but it missed the saloon and I found myself being towed along in a full-lock slide in the ERA with no way of controlling my destiny, other than keeping my eyes on the rope and trying to follow it and not let it go slack. There was no point in looking where the Bugatti was going: I just had to keep my eyes fixed on the rope. More by luck than judgement, it all came straight, but a fair amount of grass verge had passed under our wheels. At the time I was far too busy to be frightened but afterwards I was in a bit of a sweat, not so much the thought of an accident but at how we would have told the owner we had crashed his ERA.

Not surprisingly, I suppose, Michael had no qualms about asking me to be towed back to London in the Carrera, the most expensive Porsche on AFN's books in those days. Before we tied the rope on, Michael had a look around the car and spotted the trouble in an instant. Jon Pertwee did not know Porsches very well at the time and no-one had told him what to do when the petrol level got down to reserve. Down by your feet was a manually operated petrol tap hanging down from the scuttle mounted petrol tank. On the normal Porsche, petrol flowed by gravity to the pump on the engine, which raised it to the carburettors, but on the Carrera a low head of petrol in the tank needed the extra push from an electric petrol pump, due to the increased flow needed for the double-choke carburettors. With the tank full, the head of petrol was sufficient to keep the mechanical pump on the engine well fed, but when you got down to reserve you not only had to turn the tap but to switch on the electric pump. Pertwee had run down to reserve, remembered about the electric pump having to be switched on, but forgotten about turning the tap, so the engine had run dry and died. Michael turned the petrol tap lever, switched on the pump, and the car started instantly. I was in luck. Instead of a tedious tow back to London, I had the job of driving the Carrera back, which was my first introduction to Dr Fuhrmann's incredible flat-4-cylinder engine with four camshafts and 7,000rpm available.

Later I got to know Jack Burke, who bought a green Carrera, and he let me drive it quite a bit and also use it in some sprints and hill climbs, which I mention elsewhere. In fact, I got to know that car as well as my own car, and it always was a joy to drive, for the 4-camshaft engine was very much a racing unit with that lovely hard, purposeful feel of a competition engine. Jack had

The Carrera

Jack Burke's hard-used 1,500-cc Carrera, minus bumpers, when it was very active in sprints and hill climbs in the 1950s.

the standard Solex carburettors changed for double-choke Weber carburettors and I made him up a four-into-one Sebring type exhaust system. That Carrera was one of those cars that you judge to be very fast on the open road because of the amount of time you spend with the brakes really hard on, trying to stop for the next obstacle. With a normal or Super 1600 Porsche, you hardly ever used the brakes really hard on a fast cross-country run, but with a Carrera you had to if you really used its full potential.

I have mentioned in other chapters the various factory Carreras that I had the opportunity of driving, mostly on the open road, for in those days the best GT competition car was easily able to cope with normal road conditions. Today, things are vastly different and the equivalent car would be the 935 Turbo, which would be almost impossible to drive on normal roads. This change is due partly to the general advances made in automobile engineering and the sophistication brought into the design of the pure competition car, but even more to the change that has come over competitions. With the demise of the open-road motor races, like the Mille Miglia, the Targa Florio, the Panamericana Mexico and the Tour of Sicily, there is no need for a competition car to be usable under normal road conditions. With sports and GT races confined to permanent tracks, which have become smoother and

A wolf in sheep's clothing. A brand new Carrera 2, with 2,000-cc engine, outside the Porsche factory after preliminary road-testing, awaiting its bumpers.

easier over the years, the competition car has become much more specialized, finally evolving into a pure track-car, taken to and from the circuits in a transporter like a thoroughbred horse.

Similarly, that other great sporting activity, rallying, which bred the rugged GT cars like the original Carrera, has changed beyond all recognition. Today rallies are mostly held on 'special stages', either on closed roads or on private rough tracks, and these events have bred special rally cars that bear little or no relation to a racing GT car, and vice-versa. In the days of events like the Rome-Liège-Rome Rally, run on normal European roads, or the Alpine Rally through the mountains, over all the passes, the most suitable car was similar to that needed for the open-road races. Thus, cars like the 356A Carrera were well suited to both types of event, and indeed Carreras chalked up an impressive list of successes in those rugged and exhausting rallies as well as in road races.

Specialization and general development has seen the gradual divergence of rallying and racing into two wildly differing activities, and the pure GT car has suffered as a result. Today's rally cars are probably faster and more powerful than specialist racing cars, while today's racing cars require specialist drivers, and there is no room for anything in the middle. However, all is not lost, for while the family Eurobox like a VW Golf GTi has the performance of yesterday's production sports car, today's production sports car, like the Porsche 928S or the 944, has the performance of what used to be a factory sports/racing car, together with all the luxury refinements of a touring car. Even so, I still regret the loss of the opportunity to use a factory competition GT car on the normal road, for cars like the 2-litre Carrera had enormous character and were a lot of fun.

Chapter SEVEN

Competitions

It was inevitable really. Even with the cooking *'Damen'* Porsche, I could not keep away from some sort of competitive motoring, and as I have mentioned I had two friends to encourage me in Steve Wilder and Michael Burn. The first thing to do was to remove the bumpers and the hub-caps and join the Porsche team for the 1956 Six Hour Relay Race. This was run by the 750 Motor Club on a special long circuit at Silverstone, incorporating part of the present Club circuit and the centre runway down to Club corner, where a hairpin brought you back up to the normal Club circuit. In this Relay Race the driver had to carry a sash round the circuit, preferably in the car with him, and effect a 'changeover' to another team member in the pits. It was the job of the team-manager to take the sash from the incoming car and pass it to the out-going one that was waiting with its engine running, with the driver at the wheel. My 'Continental' coupé model with its sliding sunshine roof was very convenient for this, as I could hand the sash up through the roof to Michael Burn without stopping. Michael was long and lean so he was ideally built for reaching into the Porsche for the sash. The event was not memorable for our team and we didn't win, but it was a lot of fun, which was the whole object of the exercise.

In fact we finished 21st out of 24 teams, so the fun factor far outweighed the success factor, which is as it should be in this sort of event. Looking at the entry for that event, it is interesting to see some of the names adopted by the teams. Our own, which consisted of two Carreras, a 1600 Super, a 1500 Super and a 1500 Normal, was called the Stuttgart Academicals; a team of DKW saloons were Dusseldorf Wednesday; a Le Mans Replica Frazer Nash team

A Passion for Porsches

The author handing the relay sash out through the sunshine roof of his 356A during a change-over in the 1956 Six Hours Race. The white Porsche waiting to go is Leonard Potter's 1600S (Charles Dunn).

called themselves the Hounslow Hotspurs; Edgar Wadsworth's mixed team of saloon cars were the Wadsworth Wanderers; and a team called Scuderia Throttolo Bendori were a bunch of happy characters in tuned Ford Anglias, a Prefect and a Thames van. Among the drivers were Ian Walker, John Bekaert and Jean Bloxham, who all progressed to better things. Other drivers in that event who became known in a far wider sphere of racing were Peter Ashdown, Leonard Potter, Sid Hurrell, Denis Taylor, Robin Carnegie, Alan Foster, Peter Riley and Alan Staniforth.

The weekend was more memorable to me for the fact that it involved a couple of those 17-hour days that you always say you cannot cope with but which you somehow manage by sheer enthusiasm for what you are doing. Having gone to Silverstone from Hampshire bright and early on Saturday morning, to practise and then race in the Six Hour event, and having had a convivial party at a pub on the way home, I found sleep came late. Next morning saw another early start for Steve Wilder and me, for a trip across country to Brands Hatch for a two-lap sprint meeting. Steve was in his 1500 Super and I was in the 1500 Normal. At this small club meeting we cleaned up by being first and second in the class, with Steve also getting an award for the fastest closed car overall, this being against tuned Ford Zephyrs, Jaguars and Aston Martins. In those days club sprint classes were often divided simply according to open or closed bodywork and engine capacity, and we would find ourselves pitted against fairly mundane four-seater family saloons like Hillmans, Ford Anglias and the like. Other times we would have to run in the sports class against Lotus VIs and Elvas or Triumph TR2s. We gained some and lost some, but the little Porsche coupés were always a problem in these club events, as we did not have what the continental clubs called a GT category, or Gran Turismo, which was in effect a class for closed sports cars as distinct from saloons. Often Steve would win the award for the fastest closed car against genuine four-seater saloons, but as the only alternative was the class for open cars, there was no choice. We were more interested in comparing our times for the competition overall, regardless of open or closed or even engine size, and if Steve could match the times of 2-litre TR Triumphs with his 1½-litre Porsche he was well satisfied.

For four seasons I used the Porsche whenever I could for sprints and hill

Jack Burke leaving the starting line in his Carrera at the Lydstep hill climb in South Wales in 1959, with winter barely gone, judging by the trees (author).

The tight first-gear hairpins on the Trengwainton hill climb in Cornwall were just right for the little 356A.

The author hugging the kerb round the apex of Druids Hairpin at Brands Hatch whilst driving Jack Burke's Carrera. The double number on the side is due to him sharing the car with its owner. Note the absence of bumpers and hub caps; demon tuning tweaks! (Charles Dunn).

Competitions

climbs in the south of England and Wales, from Trengwainton in Cornwall, to Bodiam in East Sussex and Brands Hatch in Kent. At the first Six Hours I ran in we met Jack Burke with his green 1,500-cc Carrera. From then on, the three of us went to many meetings together, and Jack often let Steve and me share his car as it was so much faster than ours. We all loved Porsches and delighted in flying the Zuffenhausen flag in our small club events, though we never managed first, second and third, all using the same car. With the pushrod-engined Porsches, you could flatten the throttle pedal round most bends with no qualms at all, but in the Carrera we had to drive more circumspectly and with better precision, for it had nearly twice the horsepower with not much more weight. You could easily get throttle happy and spin, but although all three of us had some hectic moments, we always managed to get back under control.

The 356 Porsches were great cars for standing starts. Since the engine was coupled directly to the gearbox and rear axle, you could let the clutch in with a bang as there was no propeller shaft to 'wind up' before the power got to the wheels. With the 1600 Super engine which I put in my car after a time, you could put on 5,000rpm and just let the clutch in as fast as you liked. The back squatted down as the swing axles swung, the wheels leant inwards and you were gone with just enough wheelspin to keep the revs up around 5,000 all the time. With the high gearing of the Porsche, some of the events found you using only first and second gears, though it often meant running to 6,200. This didn't harm the engine but gave the pushrods a bit of a rough time. The Carrera ran normally to 7,000rpm and easily to 7,500rpm, so some of the short hills could be tackled all the way in first gear. One of these was the little twisty hill at Trengwainton, in Cornwall near Mousehole, a lovely little village with a lovely name, pronounced Mauzall, rather than Mouse Hole. The hill was very short and consisted of a series of tight hairpin bends. It was great fun to flick the Porsche round with the inside wheel off the ground, spinning to keep the revs well up, and never leaving first gear.

On our way to one meeting, Jack Burke and I were running fast in convoy when we came up on an XK140 Jaguar which decided to take us on. Eventually, after quite a long dice, we got by on a long undulating road, which I suspect the Jaguar driver knew well. As we both scratched by at about 95mph, with me tucked into the Carrera's slipstream, we arrived at a hump in the road and took off. Now, when you left the ground in a 356, the rear swing axle suspension allowed the half-axles to droop and the wheels took on terrific positive camber. When you landed the suspension flattened and the wheels went to terrific negative camber, and the exhaust pipes usually hit the ground with a shower of sparks. If the road was smooth you were lucky and the car would rise up to an even keel again and all would be well, but if the road was bumpy you could get into an awful pitching motion as the rear of the car oscillated up and down about the swinging half-axles, while the wheels went from being tucked under to being splayed out. If you were really unlucky, one of the oscillations could flick the car over on to its roof. To follow a 356 through these motions was a riot of fun, and an unbelievable sight if you didn't know that the car had independent rear suspension. As we landed we both got into the dreaded swing axle oscillation, but out of phase with each other. I could see what Jack was going through and could feel what my car was doing, while the Jaguar driver must have been laughing his head off. You don't lift off or brake when this happens, but keep your foot hard down, juggle with the steering wheel and hope for the best. By sheer chance we both got away with it, and carried on with our dice. The Jaguar fell back and disappeared: the driver was either having hysterics or quite unnerved at the sight of two Porsches so nearly doing ground-loops.

I used to do a little sketch of a 356 in mid-air with its rear wheels dangling, with a big exclamation mark over the driver's head and the word 'oops!' underneath. I often used this little sketch instead of signing my name, and all my friends knew it well. About this time I had a girl-friend who taught

The earthenware dinner plate made for the author by his 'pottering' girl-friend to commemorate airborne occasions in the 356A (Geoffrey Goddard).

Competitions

pottery-making at the local art school. She experienced the manoeuvre with me on a couple of occasions and was intrigued and fascinated by the whole thing, and by Porschemania as well, come to that. She made me a splendid dinner plate in her pottery school, depicting my 356 in its airborne state with the wheels tucked in, with the pattern of a Michelin X tyre down each side, as I was using X tyres on the small back wheels. Friends used to ask me what she did, and I always replied that 'she potters'.

Over the years, with encouragement from Steve and Jack, I made small changes to my Porsche to increase its performance. One of these was to make up a four-into-one exhaust system on the lines of the Sebring system used on the 550 Spyder racing cars. I also altered the handling for hill climb and sprint purposes, by playing around with types of tyre, tread patterns, wheel sizes, shock-absorbers and steering ratio. One of my most interesting experiments was a weight reduction programme. As used on the road, complete with spare wheel and tools and so on, the car weighed 1,876lb. By removing everything that wasn't needed for a hill climb, even down to the speedometer and cable and the passenger seat, I could lose 168lb of unnecessary weight. However, this was a double-edged improvement as

A factory four-into-one 'Sebring' exhaust system, named after the race in which it was first used. The author made a similar one for his pushrod engine (author).

though it helped acceleration, it upset the handling and balance of the car on fast corners, especially if it was bumpy. The problem was an old one for sports cars, namely the unsprung weight to sprung weight ratio. All the weight came off the sprung part of the car, so that the ride and suspension characteristics were not as good as in standard form. The extra performance gained by the reduction of weight aggravated the problem as well. What was needed was a reduction in the unsprung weight in direct proportion, with alloy wheels, alloy brake parts and lighter hubs and suspension members; the spring rates should also have been changed. Steve and I were planning a big programme of fibreglass doors, engine cover and luggage lid, with perspex windows instead of glass, and we reckoned we could have reduced the weight by another 10 or even 12 per cent, but it was still from the wrong part of the car. Instead, we dropped the idea and looked for better camshafts, bigger carburettors and ports and so on. Jack's Carrera had enough power in normal competition form for the events we were doing and he was all for the fibre-glass route, but we talked him out of it.

Among the events we did in those days, one of the most enjoyable was the Sprint on the Brands Hatch short-circuit run, anti-clockwise, in the opposite direction to normal. This gave you a marvellous charge down the hill from Druids Hairpin, with a flat-out rush up Paddock Bend and full noise along the top straight. Another good one was at Abridge Aerodrome in Essex. The airfield was built on a long slope so that when the perimeter track was run anti-clockwise it made a really fast hill climb. One of the most scenic was, and still is, Wiscombe Park in Devon, which also incorporates every possible type of bend, from blind flat-out left-hander to tight first gear hairpin. As today, there were plenty of small club meetings taking place, and we often took in two at a weekend, one on Saturday and one on Sunday, so we covered quite a few miles in those competition years. Running fast in convoy with two or three Porsches was as much fun as competing, especially as we had all passengered each other at various times and knew each other's driving characteristics.

Steve and I were particularly well in tune to fast driving and enjoyed some good convoy motoring, helping each other along by leap-frogging to make gaps through traffic and covering for each other when overtaking. On one Autobahn trip, a Dutch lorry and trailer pulled out in front of us without any warning, in my experience a common trait of Dutch commercial drivers, and it put us both on to the grass verge at about 85 mph. When we passed him we didn't need any form of communication to know what we were both thinking, and in unison we got side-by-side and slowed down to the lorry's 50–55mph. He almost leant on our tails, but we didn't flinch and gradually dropped our speed, almost one mile-per-hour by one mile-per hour. As the speed dropped

Competitions

to 45mph, 40, 35, 30 and so on, we heard the lorry driver having to change down. We kept this up until he was in first gear and practically climbing out of the cab to thump us, at about 10mph. With a derisive wave we snicked into bottom gear and accelerated hard, off into the middle distance and our 85–90mph cruising speed, feeling that one lorry driver would remember the two Porsches he put on to the grass verge, as he laboriously clambered back up to his 55mph maximum.

One fascinating mountain hill climb I took part in was up a mountain pass from Austria into Yugoslavia. This was very fast and on good tarmac for the first part, but ended up on loose gravel on a 1 in 4 gradient at the top. I found my 1600 Super engine pulling about 5,200rpm in second gear up the last bit, with my throttle foot absolutely flat on the floor boards. The power just

Wiscombe Park hill climb in Devon, one of the most scenic venues and also one of the nicest to race up. The author's 356A is seen about to pass through a gateway into the wooded section of the hill (A. Hollister).

The author being given the starting flag at the Wurzenpass mountain hill climb in Austria, in what appears to be a miscellaneous class, with an Alfa Romeo SV, an Austin Healey Sprite and a Fiat saloon following. Perhaps it was a practice run (author).

The author at play in driving tests on the Nurburgring in 1958, in his 356A, 'trimmed down' without bumpers or hub caps.

76

Competitions

balanced the gradient and I hung on with fingers crossed as the rev-counter dropped to 5,100 and then to 5,000, but the car just clawed its way over the top without losing any more speed. The journey back down the course was petrifying. There were some very fast 1600 Super Porsches in Austria in those days and some good sporting drivers as well, but it was all good experience for me.

I have already mentioned the 1958 Relay Race team in which Jim Clark joined us with Ian Scott-Watson's 1600S Porsche. As well as doing some of the driving, Ian acted as team-manager and sash-changer for this event, but as things turned out I had to do the lion's share of the racing for the team, which I didn't object to at all. Jimmy started off in Ian's car, lapping the special long club circuit at an average of 2 minutes 4 seconds. Then Eddy Portman took over with his very standard 1,600-cc car; he could not better 2 minutes 24 seconds, while Jack Burke averaged around 2 minutes 12 seconds in his Carrera. I was running faster, but more erratically, fluctuating between 2

Team-manager Ian Scott-Watson awaits the arrival of the sash while the author sits in his left-hand drive 356A coupé with outstretched arm, during the 1958 Six Hour Relay Race at Silverstone.

A Passion for Porsches

minutes 7 seconds and 2 minutes 11 seconds, with one lap in 2 minutes 39 seconds! This was when I tried to outbrake and run round a black A35 Austin saloon and found myself in the corn fields. Later I discovered that it was a Speedwell-tuned A35 driven by one Graham Hill! Jimmy then had a go in the Carrera and put in some laps at 2 minutes 5 seconds, although he was being very careful as he had 'lost it' during practice. Then I had another go as Ian's car had developed an oil leak. Eddy decided he would not drive any more as he was not quick enough and was not enjoying it, so I just went on and on to the end, with a short break while Jack went out again in the Carrera. Of the 160 laps we covered as a team, I found that I had done 60, the little hard-used coupé going as well at the end as at the beginning. In fact, my first flying lap had been at 2 minutes 10 seconds and my sixtieth was at 2 minutes 9 seconds. It would be nice to be able to say that all my laps were between these two figures, showing impeccable consistency, but the truth was far from it, the variations being from 2 minutes 7 seconds to 2 minutes 14 seconds. Jimmy Clark varied by only 1½ seconds over his span of 37 laps, which is one reason why he went on to be a famous racing driver and I went on to become a famous (!) author.

The 1958 Six Hours Porsche team with (left to right) Pat Burke, Jimmy Clark, Ian Scott-Watson, Eddy Portman, Jack Burke and the author, who even today does not feel happy unless he has his trousers tucked into his socks (author).

Chapter EIGHT

The Targa Florio

One nice thing about the Targa Florio races in Sicily during the 1950s and 1960s was that the competing cars were proper two-seater sports/racing cars, and were driven from the garages and workshops to the circuit for both practice and the race. This meant that you could always get a ride in one of the cars if you talked nicely to the team-manager or the head mechanic. For a number of years I used to stay at the Hotel San Lucia in Cefalu, a few miles to the east of the circuit, and the Porsche works team also stayed there, using the large underground garage as a workshop in which to prepare the cars. Providing you were up bright and early, and were ready to go, it was possible to ride to the circuit in the passenger's seat. In 1960, when Porsche were running the Spyder RS60 cars, I got a lift with Hubert Mimmler, the head mechanic, in the car Joakim Bonnier was to race.

To be driven on the normal roads in a racing car is always satisfying. The open exhaust echoes off the walls and houses, all the people wave with excitement, and the police hold up the traffic to give the racing car a clear passage. Arrival at the pits, amid all the preparation and confusion before the start, without anyone asking for a pass, is always sheer joy. The road from Cefalu joined the circuit just below Campofelice di Rocella, and we then had the 6 kilometre straight alongside the railway and the sea, to the fast corners before the pits at Cerda. Not a long ride, but one well worth taking, crouched down in the tiny cockpit in the regulation bucket seat, with the wind tearing at my bare head. Naturally Mimmler did not extend the car fully, but being the mechanic in charge of preparation he was all for making sure it was running right. Along the straight, we went up to something

A factory Porsche Spyder RS60 at a time when full-width windscreens were mandatory. Note the head-fairing behind the driver and the standard design of wheel (author).

like125mph, the hard sound of the 4-camshaft Carrera engine wafting out behind us.

As it turned out, the car in which I had opted to ride to the circuit proved to be the winning car, Jo Bonnier and Hans Herrmann sharing the driving for 7 hours 33 minutes 8.2 seconds to win the race at 95.334kph. After their long and tiring day's work, the two drivers returned to the Hotel San Lucia in the car, so I cadged a ride back in one of the other RS60s, this time in the one that had finished fifth, driven by Edgar Barth and Graham Hill. They had gone back in a road-going Porsche coupé and my old friend Herbert Linge was taking their racing car back for them. Linge had been driving in the race, sharing a new Abarth aluminium-bodied GT Carrera with his friend Paul Strahle. They had finished sixth and won the GT category. As Paul was taking the Abarth car back, Herbert agreed to take the RS60. This ensured that my ride back was equally as satisfying as the ride out, for Herbert was a hard racing driver who got on with the job. As the RS60 had finished the race in fine order, and he was ready for a bath, he wasted no time in getting back to the hotel in Cefalu. At the end of a race day, everyone on the island is still full of race-fever, so I really enjoyed the trip. To get involved in a race, however mildly, makes all the difference to one's enjoyment of the event, and the Targa Florio was the one race in which it was the easiest thing in the world to become involved in some way or another.

The previous year had seen the Porsche factory running a new version of

The Targa Florio

The author sitting comfortably outside a bar in the village of Campofelice di Rocella, watching a Porsche 910 passing down the main street during practice for a Targa Florio (Peter Coltrin).

Contrast in transportation. The factory Carrera borrowed for a blast round the Sicilian mountains, being overtaken by some local transport (author).

the GT Carrera coupé in the Targa Florio. This model was the ultimate in the development of the basic 356 'beetle' Porsche and used the 4-camshaft flat 4-cylinder racing engine. The two Barons, or, as the Sicilians called them 'Il due Barone', Antonio Pucci from Palermo, and Huschke von Hanstein, the Porsche racing manager, shared a factory car and finished third overall, behind two sports/racing Porsches from the factory. Those three splendid-sounding German drivers, Strahle, Mahle and Linge, were fourth in a similar car. Their names are pronounced Strarler, Marler and Linger, so that over the public address system they sounded a bit like a firm of solicitors or a musical group! In fact, they were three very experienced Porsche drivers who excelled on difficult circuits like the Nurburgring, the Solitudering and the Targa Florio, or in long-distance rallies like the Liège-Rome-Liège. Paul Strahle had a VW/Porsche agency near Stuttgart, Herbert Linge worked in the Porsche racing department, and Eberhard Mahle was a son of the Mahle family famous in Stuttgart as engineers and piston manufacturers. Thus, the three of them knew more than enough about racing engines, racing cars and hard driving.

    On the morning after the race, I got up bright and early with Jesse Alexander, as von Hanstein had agreed to lend us the works Carrera for a couple of hours, just as it had finished the race the day before. We went off

The Targa Florio

up into the mountains through which the Targa Florio is run and really enjoyed ourselves. As the Targa Florio circuit consists of 40 miles of winding, twisting, climbing and descending mountain roads, with a 4-mile straight forming the base of a triangle, this Porsche had been fitted with a very special gearbox in which first, second and third gears were very close, as close as on a racing motorcycle, so that you could keep the engine spinning round at nearly 8,000rpm through all the twists and turns. Fourth gear was very high and a big step away from third, but the idea was that you used it only on the long sea-level straight. On our way round the circuit we pulled 7,500rpm in fourth gear along the straight, which was well over 120mph, but the real joy was up in the mountains, using the lower three gears.

On the way back to Cefalu, Jesse unfortunately hit a stray dog. Luckily, it did no more damage than to break a sidelamp glass, but von Hanstein was quick to point out that he and Pucci had driven the car for 14 laps of the Targa Florio circuit without so much as putting a scratch on it. Now two journalists had smashed the sidelamp while out on a joy-ride. We had no answer to that.

Due to various complicated movements about Europe, involving some swapping of cars, Jesse and I had flown down to Palermo on this occasion, renting a Fiat 600 at the airport for local transport. Our next objective after leaving the Targa Florio was the Porsche factory in Stuttgart, but our route was a bit convoluted. We drove back to Palermo airport and after lunch flew on a local Douglas DC3 to Rome, where we changed on to a Convair and flew to Zurich via Milan. We stayed the night in Zurich and the next morning collected our Porsches from the local agents, where we had left them parked. We then drove in convoy to Stuttgart, cruising nicely at 80mph with occasional bursts (flat out) up to 105mph, this being on the normal roads through the Black Forest country before the Mannheim-Basle Autobahn was built.

We arrived at the Porsche factory just before lunch. While we were chatting with the press department people, the door opened and in came Paul Strahle and Herbert Linge, looking unshaven and a bit tired. They had driven the two Carrera GT cars non-stop from Cefalu! After we had given back the works car with its busted sidelamp, it had been repaired by the works mechanics, filled up with fuel and Herbie had taken it over. Paul was in his own Carrera GT and the two of them had driven in convoy right through Monday night, while we were asleep in Zurich. They had driven the whole length of Italy, over the Gotthard Pass, through Switzerland and up to Stuttgart, using normal roads since the Italian Autostrade only existed in Northern Italy at that time. Herbie's comment was, 'tough going, but good fun'.

A Passion for Porsches

Apart from the personal stamina of these two rugged German drivers, what impressed us was that the two cars had finished third and fourth over 14 laps of the gruelling Targa Florio circuit and without any attention had then been driven the 1,400 miles back to Stuttgart at equally high speed. In the 1950s, this was the sort of thing that convinced Porsche owners that the Zuffenhausen firm were serious about making good, reliable Gran Turismo cars, and they proved it time and time again. The factory always used the journeys to and from the Targa Florio, together with the week of open-road practice, to endurance-test various components on the road-going cars they used for transport. Consequently, it always paid off to look closely at the support vehicles in the car park at the Hotel San Lucia. While the actual racing cars in the workshop were of prime importance, there were always other things to see such as experimental brakes, wheels, exhaust systems, body panels, carburettor changes, gearbox alterations and so on. If you saw what appeared to be a normal 1600 SC or Super 90 coupé being used by one of the factory racing drivers for familiarization with the Targa Florio circuit, and if, when he got back to Cefalu, it was then wheeled into the

There was always something experimental to see in Sicily. This cast alloy wheel on a works production car was said to be 'some American speed-shop stuff'. It was the fore-runner of the production wheels for the 911S (author).

The Targa Florio

Graham Hill (centre) listens carefully as the author and Edward ('Photography in the Grand Manner') Eves discuss the chances of Porsche winning the Targa Florio. Note how the author is craftily standing on a bank so that he can look the others in the eye.

One of the Porsche factory trucks, laden with a works racing coupé, squeezes its way along the coastal road towards Messina on its way home after the 1963 Targa Florio (Peter Coltrin).

As the development of racing Porsches increased, they became less suitable for normal road use and by 1963 the factory cars were taken to Sicily for the Targa Florio on transporters. This one carries one car and all the tools and spares on the lower deck and two cars above (Peter Coltrin).

The Targa Florio

workshop, or taken round the back of the hotel, it was worth following to see what was going on. Disc brakes, 5-speed gearboxes, new rear suspension, alloy wheels and so on could all be inspected before they went into production.

On one occasion I had a ride round the 44-mile circuit with Graham Hill in a production Porsche SC fitted with experimental disc brakes. It was being used by the team-drivers as a practice car before the official practice day, and thus was getting a very thorough 'testing'. I happened to come out of the hotel as Graham was getting into this car, and when I asked if he was 'going for a lap', he replied, 'Yes: want to come?' That occasion sticks in my memory for it was the first time I used a seat belt, not for safety, but to keep me held firmly in the seat and out of the way of his arm and the gear lever, for he was driving hard and it would have been impossible to have held myself in place on the continual twists and turns. Even Graham was impressed with the production Porsche as a road car, and he was known for not mincing his words. When we got back to Cefalu, he murmured through his moustache, 'Hmm, bloody good car', which was praise indeed.

To return to our visit to the Porsche factory: after Strahle and Linge had arrived, we had lunch and then joined a convoy of twelve other Porsches, owned by local people, to go out to Stuttgart Airport to welcome home Edgar Barth, who had won the race with Wolfgang Seidel, Hans Herrmann and von Hanstein. As they got off the plane there was a ring of fourteen 356 Porsches to greet them and the sound of applause from the appreciative owners. It was all part of belonging to the Porsche 'family' and enjoying the Targa Florio to the full. When Vincenzo Florio first thought of the idea of the race, back in 1905, he intended it to be 'something different', and it retained this characteristic right through to the 1970s, when the 'do-gooders' in the sporting world brought about its demise. They considered it to be dangerous, undesirable and not in conformity with modern thinking, which was a great pity.

One of the last of the series I went to was the 1970 event, in which the Porsche factory turned up with some really exciting Targa Florio 'specials'. By this time the concept of the factory racing cars bearing relation to production cars had long gone, and the racing department was flat out to dominate the entire sports car racing scene, no matter what the race was or where the circuit was. The factory sports/racing cars were now powered by a very good flat 8-cylinder engine, still air-cooled, but a pure racing unit, with no relation to any future production engine. For the Targa Florio circuit, with its mountainous roads and tight twists and turns, they had built very short and compact cars termed the 908/3. They were so short in the wheelbase, to make them more 'dodgeable' through the sharp corners, that the driver sat right at

A Passion for Porsches

The second place Porsche 908/3 in the 1970 Targa Florio, showing the distinctive markings of the single arrow head and the sign of the club. Note the scooter from Palermo on the left, with its racing number 6 on the side, and the proximity of the spectators. No wonder it was a popular race (Porsche Archives).

the front, the engine being in the centre of the car. The pedals were actually ahead of the centre-line of the front wheels and the driver sat with his legs underneath the steering rack and pinion, the steering column being only a few inches in length. I happened to be with Brian Redman and Joseph Siffert when they first saw their car and the expressions on their faces when they looked into the cockpit were memorable. They could not believe that the Porsche racing department expected them to sit so far forward, for the front wheels seemed to be by their elbows. Four of these little bombs were entered for the race. To make recognition easier for the pit crews, the cars were painted with large arrows that ran along the top of the body, with the arrow head spilling over the front. In addition, each car was given a symbol from a pack of playing cards, so that one car had two arrows and a diamond, another had one arrow on the left and a club, the third car had one big arrow head right across the front and a spade, and the fourth car was devoid of an arrow head but had a heart on the right front corner.

Naturally, I was fascinated by these Targa Florio 'specials' and simply had

The Targa Florio

to cadge a ride in one, just to experience sitting that far forward. I prevailed upon Brian Redman to take me out to the circuit on race morning. Even with my small stature there was not much room in the cockpit, and I doubt if I could have survived a full lap. The blast along the 6-kilometre straight to Cerda was very exciting, for the tiny car seemed to dart about all over the road as it followed the undulations, but it was incredibly controllable. I seemed to pick lucky again, for Redman and Siffert won the race and Pedro Rodriguez and Leo Kinnunen were second in a sister car. Although it was designed purely with the Targa Florio in mind, the 908/3 was subsequently used in other races and proved to be a highly successful design.

In my report of that race in 1970, I ended with the following remarks: '. . . 78 cars had taken part in the 54th Targa Florio over 11 laps of the 72-kilometre mountain circuit, amid a record crowd of 400,000 very excitable

The racing 8-cylinder Porsche engine with two banks of 4 cylinders horizontally opposed. The plastic cooling fan on top blows air downwards across the finned cylinder barrels and heads. Four double-choke Weber carburettors are used (Porsche Archives).

and enthusiastic Sicilians, and quite a large handful of people from other countries. Yet there are mutterings in Milan that the race is dangerous and should be altered. May the real Targa Florio live on for ever . . .' Alas, the mutterings grew and the Targa Florio as we had known it was to die within a few years. A rally-type event is still held under the illustrious name, but it can never match the excitement of the real Targa Florio with out-and-out racing/sports cars from the big factories and all the top drivers taking part.

Chapter NINE

Porsche over Europe

In the ten years I spent wandering about Europe in a Porsche, reporting all types of motor racing, I went to many interesting places and saw many interesting things not directly connected with racing, so this chapter is by way of a European travelogue and an excuse to use some interesting photographs that are not necessarily connected with Porsches. My travels took me all over France, Spain, Portugal, Germany, Austria, Italy, Sicily, Switzerland, Holland, Belgium, Denmark and Sweden, with Luxembourg, Monaco, Lichtenstein and the Isle of Man thrown in for good measure.

The trips to Sicily for the races at Siracusa and for the Targa Florio, were always interesting, and before the Autostrada del Sole was extended beyond Bologna there were three ways of getting there. One was down the middle of Italy on the Via Cassia to Rome, via Florence, Sienna and Viterbo, which was the Mille Miglia route in the wrong direction. Alternatively, you could go to Rome on the Via Aurelia, which followed the Mediterranean coast from Genoa through La Spezia, Livorno and Civitavecchia. On this route you crossed the impressive Passo di Bracco and when you were well south on the edge of the sea, you got a fine view of the earth's curvature. As you came round a bend there was a very long railway viaduct in front of you, at sea level at the foot of a hill, and you were at right angles to the coast line. Beyond the viaduct was the Mediterranean sea with nothing between you and the far distant horizon. On a clear and sunny day you got a momentary glimpse of the level line of the railway viaduct and behind it the horizon of the sea. With nothing to break the view for miles and miles in each direction, you could see that the horizon was in a long shallow curve above the level of the viaduct, which gave you a straight edge for a datum line. This incredible viewpoint was on a very fast downhill section and you came upon it very suddenly, so I never did stop and record the scene.

From Rome you took the Via Appia (yes, another Lancia model name!) to Naples and then either followed the mountain road down through the centre of Calabria, through towns like Lauria, Castrovillari and Cosenza, which was very slow but a lot of driving fun, or you could take the Mediterranean coast road through Praia a Mare and Paola. Whichever way you went, you ended up on the coast road at Gioia Tauro down to Reggio Calabria. At first I assumed that Reggio Calabria was the best place to get a ferry across the Straits of Messina, but I soon discovered there was a much better and faster ferry from Villa San Giovanni before you got to Reggio C.

An entirely different route, which was longer, but took about the same number of days from France or Switzerland, was to cross the plains of Emilia beyond Bologna to the Adriatic coast at Rimini and follow the coast road down to Pescara, Bari, Taranto, Crotone and right round the toe of Italy and up to Reggio C or Villa SG by the back door, so to speak. This was a very flat and fast road, but you had to avoid the temptation of taking a short cut across the mountains when you saw a signpost saying Villa SG 94kms, when the coast road sign read 133kms. I once took this route and never got out of second gear: it took for ever. One of the hazards of the Adriatic coast road was 'going home time' which was about 5pm, as the sun was beginning to go down. The agricultural workers went home on their huge two-wheeled horsedrawn carts, piled high with grass or wood and with a dog running along underneath. The owner was usually asleep, having been out in the fields since day-break, and anyway the horse knew the way home. You would come across these carts in the middle of the road, usually heading south with you. The sun was low by this time, casting long shadows or blinding you completely as the road turned briefly westwards: a driver's nightmare. Even after dark these carts would still be trundling quietly along, totally devoid of lights, and I'll never know why I didn't hit one of them, for there were dozens and dozens of them covering a distance of 50 or 60 miles. I can only put it down to luck and quick reflexes.

The Villa San Giovanni to Messina ferry was always interesting, from the moment it arrived. It had a blunt front and the jetty was made in the same shape, lined with thick vertical wooden piles with huge steel coil springs behind them. The captain simply drove the ferry in until it fitted, with a lot of creaking and groaning from the wood and the springs. The boat had a sort of rubber-covered bumper all round it to take the shock. Sometimes the captain made a bad shot and the boat would cannon off the wooden piles from one side to the other until it self-centred itself. There was always a

Porsche over Europe

The Messina ferry heading for the jetty at Villa San Giovanni on the mainland of Italy. It was simply driven in until it fitted (author).

'helpful Giovanni' ready to relieve you of some lire in exchange for getting your ticket for you, and the stock patter was 'hurry, hurry, no time', even when there was no ferry boat at the jetty. We did one crossing on a brand new boat, about twice the size of the regular one, from a different jetty. This was a car-ferry built for the Bari to Greece run across the Adriatic ocean. Before going into service, it was having its 'sea trials' on the Villa SG to Messina run. It took about three times as long to make the crossing, most of the time being spent manoeuvring in and out of the harbours, but we got chatting to the captain and he spent the time showing us all over his new vessel with great pride.

If you didn't have a car with you, it was possible to cross the Straits very quickly on a hydrofoil, a sort of cabin cruiser that rode up on water skis once it was underway, with only the propeller in the water. It was powered by a big Mercedes-Benz diesel engine and was good for 50 or 60mph: on the smooth waters of the Mediterranean, it was very impressive. If I was spending the night in Messina, at one of the harbour-front hotels, I often went for a quick return trip to Reggio C and back on the *Freccia d'Oro*, just for pleasure.

A Passion for Porsches

The Mercedes-Benz-powered hydrofoil Freccia d'Oro *at rest on the Messina dock-side. Once up on its water skis it travelled at some 60mph and did the crossing of the Messina Straits in ten minutes* (author).

For scenic views Sicily is superb, the countryside and mountains being so unspoilt and natural. Part of the charm of watching the Targa Florio race was the day spent in the Sicilian mountains. Over the years I must have driven on every road in Sicily, and spun my Porsche on a number of occasions, for the road surfaces were incredibly slippery at all times, almost polished, in fact. I was once told this was due to volcanic dust from Mount Etna getting into the surface, but I don't know if that is true or not.

Austria was, and still is, a good touring country, but it is very 'trim' and neat and tidy compared to Sicily. Once again, however, if you like mountain motoring – and Porsches love mountains – it is a great country for driving. In almost every country I visited there was an opportunity to deviate off the route, either to see something, to try a new route, or to visit friends. Some of the accompanying photographs illustrate such opportunities.

Every year at the Targa Florio, a peanut vendor was on duty at the Bivio Polizzi refuelling point in the mountains, arriving in a three-wheeled Vespa Scooter pick-up truck appropriately called the 'Freccia del Sud' *Arrow of the South* (author).

A Sicilian farmhouse high in the mountains somewhere on the Targa Florio circuit (author).

The author's Porsche 356A, heading for the Grossglockner pass after an Austrian hill climb meeting, pauses at a roadside shrine with typical Austrian mountains forming a back drop (author).

The author's 356A Porsche about to enter a tunnel through the Austrian Alps in the happy days of relatively traffic-free roads in Europe in 1958. You cannot imagine parking your car in a position like this today in order to take a photograph (author).

With the little 356 'beetle' Porsche there was always room to park, even if it was a bit untidy at times. The author's car is seen squeezed into a gap in a Spanish town in 1958 (author).

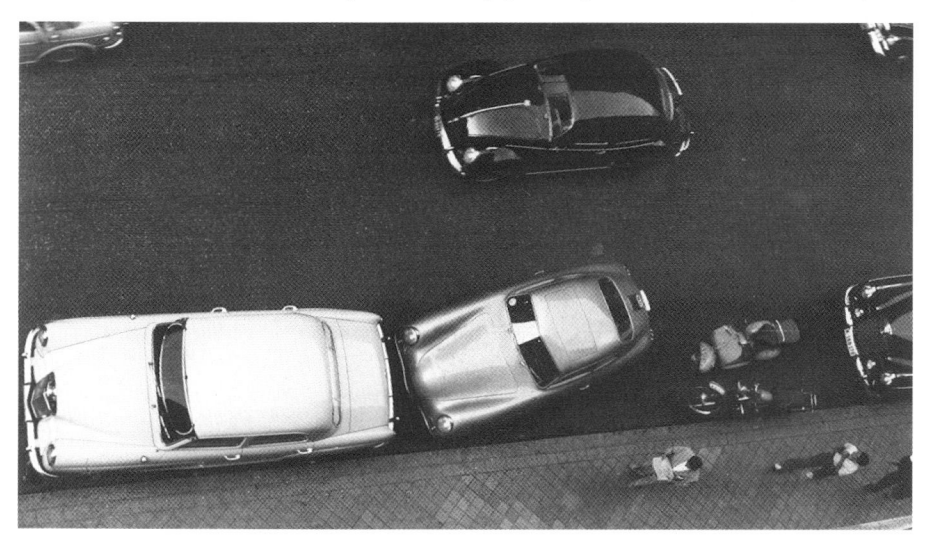

A Passion for Porsches

When spending a lot of time in Germany, I often went to local club gatherings, and one such was a lunch-time assembly at the Hockenheim circuit. Afterwards a group of us went to tea with one of the members near Mannheim and we then decided to go and visit another friend who lived in a big castle not far from Neckarsulm. In the accompanying photograph our cars are seen lined up in the courtyard outside the castle after a very spirited cross-country 'convoy dice' led by the 190SL in the foreground, its owner knowing the way. Then came the drophead 327/80 BMW, the author's Porsche, and those of von Frankenberg and Dr Biesenberger. It was one of those splendid early evening runs on winding country roads, where only the leading car knew where it was going, so the important thing was not to lose sight of the car in front. Even though the 190SL was going at a moderate pace, the tail of the convoy was flat-out. The two saloon Mercedes-Benz nearest the door were already there on our arrival, as they lived there. After an informal buffet supper and some nice Mosel wine we all went our separate ways, but it was one of those unplanned motoring days with sporting friends that makes the ownership of a car something more than mere transport (author).

Porsche over Europe

During the war in Italy one of the most bitter campaigns was that involving the monastery at Monte Cassino. The gigantic monastery stands high on a hill overlooking the little village of Cassino, and commands an incredible view of the surrounding countryside, so it was not surprising that the German forces operated from it. All around are lower hills and these were used by the British and American forces as strongpoints. I visited the area in the early 1950s and was amazed to find the monastery completely rebuilt and like new, while the village of Cassino was still in ruins. Many years later it was rebuilt, but obviously only as a second priority. On one journey back from Sicily I made a detour up the hill from which the British attack was carried out, to find these imposing steps at the top, leading up to a monument to commemorate the famous battle (author).

A Passion for Porsches

Porsche travels took me to just about every corner of Europe and one year, after a visit to the races at Lisbon, we stayed on in Portugal and went down south to stay with Luis Montero, a keen Portuguese Porsche enthusiast. His family bred fighting bulls and one day he took Peter Coltrin and me to see some of them grazing peacefully in a field. We were on the opposite side of a fairly large water-filled irrigation channel, so felt safe enough, but when Luis crossed a single plank 'bridge' into the field we hung back. Eventually we plucked up courage and crossed the 'bridge' but were very uneasy, even though the bulls had not even seen us and were pointing the other way as they grazed. Luis was all for us taking a closer look at the bulls, as he was obviously very proud of them, but we were not at all enthusiastic. Suddenly one of the bulls turned round and looked straight at us and Pete and I nearly fell in the water in our rush for the plank bridge. However, afterwards we were always able to say nonchalantly, 'Oh yes, we've been in a field with a fighting bull'. The Montero home, depicted here with the 356A and Pete outside, was much more to our liking (author).

Porsche over Europe

By the mid-1950s Germany had well and truly recovered from the aftermath of war and a new Germany was being built, with a whole new concept of architecture. During one deviation from the normal path, I visited Friedrichshafen on the edge of the Bodensee, better known as Lake Constance, and found much of the town rebuilt in the modern style shown in this photograph, though even in this modern idiom the German designers still found room for birds on the wall surrounding the clock, which was rather nice (author).

A Passion for Porsches

Crossing the Swiss Alpine passes was always very enjoyable, but not always possible, for sometimes the snow was not gone until June. Nowadays there are magnificent road tunnels through the Alps, but 20 years ago the only means of getting to the other side when the snows still closed the pass was by the train ferry. It was a very simple affair, consisting of a line of open platform-trucks joined by ramps. You drove on at one end, and off at the other, after the train had taken you through the tunnel, so first on was first off. There were no formalities: you put the handbrake on, the man put a chock under the wheels, and you sat in your car throughout the journey, which could be as long as 15 or 20 minutes. Rattling through the tunnel in complete darkness, sitting at the wheel of your car, and doing 40 or 50mph was quite unnerving, and it was no use pressing on the foot brake if you felt you were travelling too fast. Illustrated is the train ferry about to set off through the Gotthard tunnel (author).

If I took a friend from England with me on a trip to Sicily, I would call in at Modena and Peter Coltrin would accompany us in his Porsche. Here the two cars are seen resting in the Sicilian sunshine when we stopped for a splendid sea-food lunch on the coast between Messina and Palermo. You could sense in some of the small restaurants along the coast that the fish had been in the sea that very morning; there was no problem with transport, it was just a case of carrying the fish from the beach to the kitchen. It is interesting to compare the 356A on the left of the picture with the 356B on the right, illustrating how the B-series was slightly taller, had a single curvature windscreen in place of the single piece vee screen, a deeper windscreen and slimmer roof line. The front bumper of the B was American-style, with taller over-riders and an extra bar. I thought my rubbing strips bolted directly on to the body were much nicer looking and just as ineffective (author).

I always enjoy looking down on motor cars, for that way you get a much better appreciation of their lines. Some manufacturers look at their prototype models from all angles, others only from ground level, while judging by the shape of some cars you would think they were designed in the dark and no-one looked at them until they were in production. The Porsche 356A was always a pleasure to look at from on high, and as there was a saying in Porsche mythology that 'there is only one thing better than a Porsche: two Porsches', this photograph taken from the balcony of a friend's flat in Bruxelles was a 'must'. Close scrutiny will show that I was better at parking than he was! (author).

A Passion for Porsches

Porsche over Europe

Left:
As the years went by, the Autostrada del Sole was gradually extended right to the toe of Italy, and in many places in Calabria it replaced the existing road rather than supplemented it, which is why there are no tolls in the deep south. During my travels I saw much of the building in progress through the mountains of Calabria. The concrete tower illustrated was something like 240 feet high. It was one of a row being built across a huge valley to carry the Autostrada as a viaduct across the valley. I had wound my way down one side and was about to climb up the other. Today, you can travel the Autostrada on a level road without knowing how far from the ground you are, which is just as well in some places. When you see Italian civil engineering feats like this, you have to admit that not all Italians are irresponsible and scatterbrained! However, a nice touch in this instance was a 'plumb-line' dangling from the upper structure down to within a foot of the ground. It was a length of string with a rock tied on the end. No matter from where you viewed that tower and the plumb-line, it was spot-on for being vertical. You can't beat mother nature and gravity (author).

The final photograph in this interlude from the serious business of Porsches and driving them was taken at the Zuffenhausen factory and shows a line of 356C coupés awaiting collection. You would often find a line-up like this, with all the cars fitted with temporary export Zoll plates, awaiting the arrival of a group of American owners. Such communal deliveries were usually tied in with a trip by the Porsche Club of America, and the owners would either drive back to Le Havre or Cherbourg and sail home, or they would stay for a touring holiday in Europe and return home from Genoa or Naples by boat (author).

Chapter TEN

Brief Encounters

Even when not on a Porsche trip, you seem to come across them and be influenced by Zuffenhausen, and it was ever thus, especially in sporting circles in which I have always moved. In 1955 I went to Sweden for the Sports Car Grand Prix at Kristianstad. At the time, I was very wrapped up in Mercedes-Benz, even though I drove up to Scandinavia in my 1500 Porsche coupé. After the Grand Prix there was a small race meeting in the middle of Sweden at Karlskoga, so having nothing else to do I went there to watch the fun. It was nothing more than a club meeting really, on a tiny little track built outside the town, and as I was wandering about in the paddock during practice I came upon Wolfgang von Trips, sitting in a factory 300SL Gullwing Mercedes-Benz. He had raced one of these cars the previous weekend and had come to Karlskoga more for a holiday than anything else. He told me he had to deliver one of the factory 300SL coupés back to Stockholm after this race meeting, but had the use of it for a week and was planning to drive up to the north of Sweden in it. He concluded by saying, 'Do you know anyone who would like to come with me?' Well, I ask you, what would you have said? It took but a few minutes to make arrangements of my own and then I was able to say to him, 'When do we start?'

At the Karlskoga races, Wolfgang had met the Stockholm Mercedes-Benz agent to whom he had to deliver the car, and he had told him he was about to go on holiday and would not be back in the capital city for a whole week. The agent suggested that von Trips might like to keep the car and use it in the interim if he was not in a hurry to return to Germany. Now von Trips was a young man who enjoyed life to the full and had an adventurous spirit, so

Brief Encounters

as soon as I said I would join him, he outlined his plan. This was simply to keep driving north and see what happened, Sweden being a very big country. It sounded a super idea and we had seven full days in which to achieve it, for our dead-line was 8am on the morning of Monday week.

At the Karlskoga races were André Loens and his friend Geoff Holyoak. André was racing his A6G Maserati sports car, which he and Geoff carried about in an old motor coach converted into a transporter. They were due to race at the Roskildering in Denmark the following weekend, so while Geoff was to drive the coach, André agreed to take my Porsche and drive it to Denmark. The plan was that he could use it for transport during the weekend and then, before they left on Monday morning, leave it in the car park of the BP Motel near the entrance to the Roskilde track, leaving the keys with the girl at the reception desk. I reckoned I would be back by Tuesday and could pick up the car from there. Just how I was going to get from Stockholm to Roskilde I had no idea, but that was a problem for the future; the main thing was to get organized for Monday.

The prize-giving party after the races was one of the good ones, with drinking and dancing going on until 3 in the morning. At one point Ken Tyrrell, who in those days was racing a Formula 3 Cooper-Norton, strode over to a grand piano and with a great flourish pounded out the opening bars of a Rachmaninoff Piano Concerto. We all sat back, thinking, 'This is going to be nice', at which Ken got up, walked away from the piano, and said, 'That's all I know.'

After a few hours' sleep, I got up to find Geoff wandering about in the ballroom looking rather lost. He was in his shirt-sleeves, with his trousers held up by a tie round his waist, and he was looking for his braces. Somehow they had become lost during the party and he felt they must be somewhere around. Eventually we found them, dangling from an enormous glass chandelier hanging from the ceiling in the centre of the ballroom. It was still relatively early, no-one was about, and we were not in a very bright state, certainly not able to think about things like step-ladders. We cast around the room and came up with a table and a chair, but even Geoff's 6 foot 2 inches was not enough to reach the chandelier. So, while he stood on the table, I stood on his shoulders, and with the aid of a broom I managed to unhook his braces from amongst the myriad of lamp bulbs and globes. With a great sigh of relief, we all collapsed on to the floor without bringing the whole chandelier down. It really is amazing what you can do when you are up against it. If we hadn't seen the braces up on the chandelier, Geoff would have probably been quite happy with a piece of string to replace his tie, but finding them presented that sort of challenge.

It was a bit like another late-night party when an ornamental garden statue

The racing 300SL Mercedes-Benz, with its gull-wing doors open, is seen on a typical Swedish dirt road through a forest. It was quite happy at 70–75mph on such going. It still wears its racing number from the Karlskoga meeting (author).

ended up at the bottom of the deep end of a swimming pool at an Italian hotel. When the party finished, we felt honour-bound to replace the statue, knowing exactly where it was, but fishing it up out of the deep end was no easy matter. By joining together a whole collection of leather belts, ties and bits of string, another chap and I were able to dive down and tie the line on to the statue's arms and a concerted team effort got it safely back up on to dry land. By this time most of those involved had ended up in the pool, fully clothed, and as we dripped our way out of the hotel across a marble floor, we said goodnight to the long-suffering manager and apologized for the water across the floor. 'Don't worry', he said, 'It is my water, from my pool.' A very nice, understanding man.

To return to the Swedish epic: it was midday before Wolgang and I were ready to leave and André had taken charge of my Porsche. The 300SL was a competition version with little in the way of creature comforts, running on Continental racing tyres and still carrying its Karlskoga race numbers. We took the minimum of luggage and the maximum amount of money we could borrow from various friends, and set off. That car really came alive at 4,100rpm, and then went like smoke. It cruised happily on the dirt roads at 75 mph with Wolfgang driving, and frequently topped 100mph. With a

While Wolfgang von Trips chats with the owner of the Porsche encountered in the far north of Sweden, the owner's wife and 12-year-old daughter take the opportunity to feed the 18-month-old baby that travelled in the back of the 356A (author).

normal driver I would have been petrified, as the car skated about on the dust and loose stones, but von Trips was no ordinary driver. He was good enough to be in the Mercedes-Benz sports car team and was later to join the Ferrari Grand Prix team. When he went as fast as he felt was safe on the dirt roads, we clocked 110mph, but it was getting a bit dodgy, and he settled for 100mph as the usable maximum. On good tarmac roads, and there were some in Sweden, 125mph was a good cruising speed even with the low Karlskoga gearing, and we did this quite a bit on the return trip to Stockholm. The dust clouds out behind the Mercedes were unbelievable and for that matter so were the dust clouds inside the car, for as it was a competition model the sealing was minimal. Every now and again we had to slow down and have a 'blow through' which involved opening all the vents, raising both gullwing doors, removing the two rear quarter windows and going along slowly until all the dust had dispersed. Then we would seal everything up as well as we could and blast on again. Of course, we could have gone slowly all the time and not raised the dust, but that would have been a waste of a good car and not so much fun.

Although Wolfgang was a works Mercedes-Benz driver, he was still a Porsche enthusiast at heart and still ran his own 1500 Super. On our third day

A Passion for Porsches

going north we caught up with a German registered Porsche and both whooped with joy, for in those days that far north there was not much traffic to see, let alone another 'tourist' and in a Porsche at that. Wolfgang overtook the Porsche and waved it down. The owner came from Braunschweig and had his wife and two children with him, all in a normal 1500 Porsche. His wife and 12-year-old daughter were sharing the passenger seat while their 18-month-old baby was in a carry-cot on the platform behind the seats, and most of their luggage was on a rack on the tail. We compared notes of where we had been and where we were going, and what it had been like, and we told him about the dust in the 300SL and how we had to have a 'blow through' every now and then. Taking us over to his Porsche, he said, 'My Porsche is perfect, look'. We looked with amazement into the little coupé, for it was immaculate and they had come on the same route as us, but no doubt at a lot

Within sight of the line of the Arctic Circle, the Mercedes-Benz punctured another tyre and we had no more spares. It was Hobson's choice to remove the tyre and drive slowly along on the rim (author).

more leisurely pace. He was as enthusiastic about Porsches as we were, so we passed a happy time before climbing into our dust-bowl and charging off into the tundra.

We were now pretty far north and had the mad idea of crossing into Norway, going up into the Arctic Circle, round the top of Sweden into Finland, then southwards and taking a ferry across the Baltic back to Stockholm. We crossed into Norway as planned, drove on up into the Arctic Circle and 200 miles further north stopped for the night at the coastal village of Bodö. Unfortunately our super plan had to be abandoned, for when we studied the map we found the next leg of the journey was going to involve a lot of ferry crossings of fiords and the people in the hotel told us how long it would take. We debated for a long while but what finally put us off was when we looked at the tyres on the Merc: the back ones were bald. That far north it only got dark for about half an hour and we stayed up late just to see if it was really true. At 11.30pm we could still see to read a newspaper out in the street, and by midnight it was getting light again, while by 12.30am it was broad daylight.

Reluctantly we had to retrace our steps, and before we got back to the line of the Arctic Circle our right rear tyre punctured, the cover being worn right through. We put on the spare and just as we got to the notice board proclaiming the line of the Polar Circle, our left rear tyre wore through and deflated. As the sun was shining and it was beautifully warm, there was only one thing to do, and that was to take some photographs and have a sandwich from our ration box. With no spare tyre we had little choice, so using what tools we could find we removed the worn out tyre and motored on the rim at low speed until we found a garage with a bicycle puncture outfit, which was 20 kilometres on. As he drove gingerly along, Wolfgang laughed and said, 'Like Sir Henry Birkin in the Bentley at Le Mans'. His knowledge of racing history was good, like all German racing enthusiasts.

By some pretty heroic motoring, we got the Mercedes-Benz back to Stockholm by Sunday night and duly delivered it next morning after giving it a good wash. Apart from the tyres, you would not have known it had been well up into the Arctic Circle. Wolfgang got a plane back to Stuttgart and I flew to Copenhagen, where I then got a taxi to the railway station and a train to Roskilde and walked to the motel to pick up my Porsche. I was a bit concerned when I did not see my little blue coupé in the car park, but went in and asked the girl at the desk, whom I knew from previous visits, if she had the keys of my car. She hadn't and furthermore knew nothing about my car or about it being left for my collection! André and Geoff had been at the races and had stayed at the motel, and she had been on duty all the time, but there had never been any mention of a

Count von Trips seated on the 'sill' of the gull-wing-door racing Mercedes-Benz 300SL in Sweden during this trip to the Arctic Circle with the author. We still had tread on the tyres at this point! (author).

The young Count von Trips poses by the signboard indicating that we had arrived at the Arctic Circle in the racing 300SL Mercedes-Benz. This was while we were still travelling northwards with four inflated tyres and a spare. The next day on the return trip was a very different story (author).

Brief Encounters

Porsche and she did not recall seeing one. To say that I was baffled was to put it mildly.

It was nearly lunchtime, so there was only one thing to do, and that was to have lunch and do some serious thinking. Either André had left the car at Karlskoga for some reason, or he still had it but had changed the plan. There was no message anywhere in the motel and all the racing people had left, so there I was, in the middle of Denmark, with no transport and fast running out of money, with no idea where my car was. I spent all afternoon on the telephone to various people and eventually discovered that Geoff Holyoak had returned to England, but since he had not gone home his wife had no idea where he was. André had gone to Roubaix but nobody knew exactly where. By early evening I gave up and decided I would stay at the motel, which was very friendly and comfortable anyway, until something happened or I had a bright idea. Next morning, while I was having breakfast, I was told I was wanted on the telephone, and there was a man saying, 'Mr Jenkinson, I have your Porsche' – relief!

He arrived in time to stay to lunch with me and the car was looking immaculate, having been washed and polished. It turned out that he had been talking to André who told him about the plan to leave the car in the motel car park. He was horror-struck: 'No', he said, 'I will take it to my house and keep it in my garage; there it will be safe.' André had given him the keys after the meeting and he took it home on Sunday night. No one had thought to tell the girl at the desk as I had said I would be back on Tuesday and he planned to ring the motel first thing Tuesday morning, before I arrived. For once in my life I arrived somewhere early, and look what happened! I have always thought it better to arrive late than not at all. Arriving early has never been my strong point.

After taking my Danish friend back to Copenhagen, I set off down through Denmark and into Germany, heading for the Nurburgring and the next race. I see in my motoring log that I arrived safely at Adenau having put 77 miles into one hour on the Hannover-Dusseldorf Autobahn and witnessed two enormous lorry crashes. Obviously the Porsche had not suffered while it was 'lost'. Next day I lapped the Nurburgring a number of times in just over 14 minutes a lap, and then took Jean Behra round for some laps while he memorized the circuit, after which he took me round in his Lancia Aurelia Spyder.

Mention of Jean Behra reminds me of what a Porsche enthusiast he was. He drove for the works team many times, and regrettably killed himself at the AVUS track in a Porsche Spyder. When he was with the Porsche team, Jean used a 1600S as a road car. I remember stopping for petrol at the Porsche agent in Reims to find him out the back in the workshop, making a new steering column for his car – a new coupé that he had just driven from Stuttgart.

Jean Behra's Lancia Aurelia 'Spyder' that he used for travel about Europe during 1955. He used it to learn circuits before practice began and took the author round the Nurburgring in it (author).

Jean Behra, in crash-helmet, behind the car, explains his single-seater Porsche to a group of officials during practice for the Pau Grand Prix in 1959. The car was very neat and slim and was built around a tubular space-frame designed by Valerio Colotti (author).

Brief Encounters

He found that the steering wheel was too close to him and so he ripped the whole lot out. When I found him, he was busy with hacksaw and welding plant making up a column that was 2 inches shorter. It doesn't sound much, but to a fastidious driver like Jean Behra everything had to be right. If anyone has an old Porsche today in which the steering wheel is 2 inches closer to the scuttle than it should be, it is probably ex-Behra. Having short arms I was not troubled by this, but I did suffer from pedal length, having short legs, and very early on I made up some lengthened pedal stalks, putting a particularly long one on the clutch pedal to aid me with standing starts in sprints and hill climbs.

Later on Jean Behra was to construct his own single-seater Formula 2 Porsche, long before the factory did the same. He was living at the Hotel

Graham Hill adjusts his left-hand mirror before setting off for practice at the Nurburgring in a factory Formula 2 Porsche in 1960. The factory cars had a detachable panel on the nose for getting at the pedals and brake gear, while the Behra car had a completely detachable nose, the engine in both cars being behind the driver (author).

A Passion for Porsches

When you saw this large Mercedes-Benz transporter at a race meeting during the 1960s, you knew that the Porsche factory team had arrived. It is seen in the paddock at Le Mans (author).

Reale in Modena at the time and Valerio Colotti had left the Maserati design office and set up on his own. Behra produced a sports/racing two-seater RSK which they took apart, and Colotti designed a single-seater tubular spaceframe to which all the Porsche mechanical components were fitted. The resultant car was called the Behra-Porsche and was painted French blue. As I was also spending a lot of time in Modena in those days, I watched the construction of this car with interest and occasionally helped Jean on small jobs. When it was all done, he took it to the Modena Aero-Autodromo to try it out and run it in. He let me go along and drive it round for a lap, just to see if everything worked properly.

It was a very neat and compact little car and the Porsche factory were not very pleased, as they were thinking about the same idea. When their Formula 2 car appeared, it was nothing like so neat and compact as the Behra car. Recently, the Behra-Porsche has been resurrected and it now takes part in historic racing.

Brief Encounters

Like the author, the Italian engineer Valerio Colotti was of normal height! They are chatting in front of the offices of Gear Speed Developments, a firm started by Colotti with the well-known mechanic Alf Francis. It was Valerio Colotti who designed the chassis for the Formula 2 Porsche that Jean Behra constructed out of a Spyder RSK sports car (Peter Coltrin).

A Passion for Porsches

The author learning about body-building from Merdardo Fantuzzi in Modena who made all the Maserati and Ferrari racing bodies. He was also very helpful in straightening out the ravages of European travel on the author's 356A Porsche (Peter Coltrin).

The Modena coachbuilder Fantuzzi was always being asked to repair the ravages of travel on the author's Porsche. This crumpled side was the result of an altercation with a 4cv Renault in the French Alps (author).

Chapter ELEVEN

Of the Porsche kind

I seldom passed Stuttgart during the 1950s without calling in at the Porsche factory, either to buy the odd spare part, or merely to say hello. Quite often the visits proved more than worthwhile, as they coincided with the opportunity for a brief run in something interesting. One of these occasions was shortly after a Targa Florio race when the factory-entered Carrera coupé was standing in the yard out behind the racing department. At this time I had not driven a factory Carrera, so I enquired whether there was a chance of having a go in one. The only one available was the one in the yard, but there was a snag. It had no doors, by which I do not mean that the sides were sealed up: they just were not there. This particular year's Targa Florio had been used to test some aluminium doors on the Carrera coupé. They had been taken off on its return from Sicily, and were in the inspection and test department, being given a thorough going-over by the engineers to see how they had stood up to the trip to Sicily and back and competing in the race. The Porsche people said, 'If you don't mind taking it as it stands, borrow the Targa Florio car for the afternoon.' The lack of doors did not worry me unduly as the racing bucket-seat held me very firmly in place, so I accepted gratefully and zoomed off out through the back of Zuffenhausen and up to the Autobahn.

Any Carrera Porsche, with its racing 4-camshaft engine, is exciting to drive, and this works model was even more so, as you knew that the engine was safe at 7,000rpm and more if you needed it. It was that much sharper than a production Carrera and made a lovely noise with its four-pipes-into-one 'Sebring' exhaust system. If I had not been in a car carrying factory Stuttgart

Of the Porsche kind

number plates, I might have been a bit embarrassed by the noise, but anywhere around Stuttgart a factory Porsche was known for what it really was, a pure racing car, even though it was a road-going coupé. After a quick blast down the Autobahn to enjoy the terrific surge up to 100mph and then way on beyond, to 120–125mph, which was something a normal 1600S did not do, I turned off and went to the Solitude circuit, in the hills to the south-west of Stuttgart. Although it was always known as the Solitude circuit, it was all part of the normal road system around that area, but for many years the roads were closed once a year for car and motorcycle races. It thus became a permanent circuit, in effect, with permanent pits and time-keeping house, and was always kept in good condition. Apart from one or two road junctions where you had to watch out for traffic, you could really use the Solitude as a race-track even though the roads were open, so it was a favourite haunt of anyone from the factory in those days. I had a marvellous time dicing round and round the Solitude, for I knew it very well, having raced motorcycles and sidecars there for a number of years.

 Driving that works Carrera without doors really was an amusing experience, and there was certainly no shortage of elbow room to work away on the steering as I *'wischened'* round some of the swerves. In the lower gears up the steep climb after the start, the Carrera really flew, for it had been geared especially for the mountains of Sicily. In a car like that you had only a rev-counter to look at, for though a speedometer was fitted it was merely academic as the speedo head bore little relation to the axle ratio. Porsche have always insisted that the rev-counter is the most important instrument on which to drive a car and the works Carrera was no exception. The needle whizzed round to 7,500rpm phenomenally quickly, with that lovely hard noise from the engine, the firm push on the back of the seat and a gear change that was as quick as you could move the lever. After many laps of the Solitude, which is one of my favourite circuits, I then went off into the lovely countryside south of Stuttgart for some 'fast touring', before returning by way of the Autobahn for a last glorious blast as far as the Zuffenhausen turn-off. In spite of being to racing specification, the car was entirely flexible and docile and poodled back into Zuffenhausen and round to the back of the racing department like a Volkswagen. That was fun.

 Towards the end of 1959, I went off to compete in a mountain hill climb in Austria. On the way back, I called in at the factory to pass the time of day, only to discover that the Porsche Club of America had arrived en masse, many of them to pick up brand new Porsches and to join the International Porsche Rally in Switzerland. It was my luck once again that everyone was about to go out to the Solitude for a test afternoon. The factory had arranged to have the roads closed and had laid on a collection of cars for demonstration, so

A Passion for Porsches

When the author called in on a Porsche Club gathering on the Solitude circuit, he was taken for a ride in a Spyder RSK racing/sports car by Huschke von Hanstein and later was let loose in it on his own (Meisinger).

naturally I joined in. Many of the Americans were driving a Porsche for the first time, so this was a grand opportunity for them to learn about their cars. I spent a lot of the afternoon giving 'demonstrations' in my own car and in the factory production cars, as well as taking some of the owners in their cars.

Among the 'demonstrators' in the line-up was a Targa Florio GT Carrera, by now a 2-litre, and also an RSK Rennsport, a factory sports/racing car. I had Pete Coltrin with me, as he was collecting his own car from the factory service department, and I took him for a run in the Carrera GT, as he had never been in one. Needless to say, as a Porsche owner he was impressed, but he admitted that even had he not been a Porsche owner, he would have been impressed. A car like the Carrera GT was about my personal limit of performance. I could use it to the full and 'play bears' almost to the point of losing it and spinning off, though I never did. Consequently I revelled in the opportunity to dice round the Solitude when it was closed to normal traffic.

Before the end of the afternoon Huschke von Hanstein took me for a few

Of the Porsche kind

laps in the RSK. This was a different world for me, for though the engine did not give much more power than the Carrera GT, the whole car was much lighter, had better road holding and was much more 'nervous' and responsive to skill with the controls. After my demonstration run, von Hanstein got out and said, 'You take it.' It was really more than I could cope with, for while I drove it as hard as I could, I knew that I was not using the full potential of the car, something you do not appreciate until you have been with someone who can. Even so, it was an opportunity not to be missed, and in fact presented a perfect situation for my analytical mind regarding the subject of motor racing. Having seen what the car could do, I could easily see where I was lacking, and it was mostly in bravery. Even though I knew a certain corner to be flat-out in fifth gear, for von Hanstein had shown me, I could not bring myself to do the same-which is the difference between a writer/enthusiast who can drive racing cars and a racing driver who can write articles. Nonetheless, I enjoyed the experience of the RSK to the full, and looking back into my 1959 log-book I see I wrote a brief but poignant note – 'Drove the RSK (Wow!)'.

Eventually this splendid impromptu afternoon ended. While everyone else returned to their hotel to wash and polish in readiness for a dinner/reception that evening at the magnificent Schlöss Solitude, I got into my much-travelled 356A coupé and set off for Paris, arriving there at 1.30am. I could not 'play' all the time: I had to be at work the next day, reporting the Paris Salon for my magazine and then reporting on the Sunday races at the Linas-Montlhéry Autodrome.

Now that the competition Porsches were represented both by the Carrera GT coupé and by the RSK open two-seater, the time had to come for an amalgamation of the two. The Spyder Porsches had the racing 4-camshaft engine mounted centrally, ahead of the rear axle, while the Carreras still adhered to the 356 layout with the engine behind the rear axle. What obviously had to come was a coupé with the engine mounted centrally, and this appeared in the form of the 904. Porsche racing philosophy was undergoing great changes around 1960/61, for whereas the firm had always raced cars that were in the line of production models, they were now beginning to relinquish that idea and develop pure racing models. Unlike previous Porsches that were built on a steel platform chassis, the 904 used two box-section side-rails and was a rigid structure without any need for strengthening by the bodywork. Consequently, a lot of the bodywork could be made of light glass-fibre. Also, the front suspension was by wishbone and coil springs and the rear suspension was fully independent with good geometry, at last breaking away from the original swing-axle design. This new car was powered by the well-tried flat-4-cylinder, 4-camshaft Spyder engine, the

A Passion for Porsches

The Porsche 904 broke new ground with a box-section chassis frame and front suspension by a wishbone system in place of the traditional Porsche trailing link system. The Carrera engine was mounted amidships instead of behind the rear axle (Porsche Archives).

racing version of the Carrera engine, and this was mounted ahead of the rear axle instead of behind it, while the body was a very small and compact two-seater coupé.

The first 904 to come to the United Kingdom was bought by Dickie Stoop, to replace his previous 356 Carrera. I was at the Phoenix Green Garage on the A30, west of Camberley, one day, when he arrived in his new acquisition, painted British racing green. Dickie was never one to take his sports/racing cars about on trailers and always taxed and insured them for use on the road. He lived at The Grange, just outside Hartley Wintney, and kept his racing cars in the family garage, using them locally like other people used their Volkswagens.

After I had crawled all over this exciting new acquisition of his, he offered to give me a ride. Climbing into the small cockpit, we closed the doors and set off down the A30, westwards beyond Basingstoke, taking the by-pass as it was then, before the M3 motorway transformed Basingstoke. On the way back Dickie shouted that he had to go into Basingstoke to do some shopping. He

Of the Porsche kind

had to shout as the noise level in the 904 was very high, with the engine close to the bulkhead behind the seats and the confined space within the cockpit. We deviated off into the town and pulled up outside a cake shop, causing quite a stir among the Ford Zephyrs and Austin Westminsters of the local farmers, for this was long before Basingstoke was transformed from a local market town into an over-spill city. Dickie disappeared into the cake shop and came out bearing a large cream cake with a sheet of tissue paper over it. He handed this to me and clambered back into the driving seat. With a shattering roar from the racing exhaust system, we set off back to Hartley Wintney, with me balancing the cream cake on my knees. At 100–120mph we returned along the A30 to adjourn at 'Stoop Towers', as we called the family home, for tea and cream cake with Dickie's mother. Meanwhile the exciting 904 coupé sat outside on the gravel drive, ticking away quietly to itself as it cooled down.

I always thought it was a pity that Porsche never made a road-going production version of the 904, even if it had been a limited run, for its concept as a sports car was absolutely right. The Porsche factory had other

Dickie Stoop's shiny new Porsche 904 with everything opened up, all the moveable panels being made of glass-fibre. The 4-cam engine was mounted between the cockpit and the rear axle.

Dickie Stoop's brand new 904 Porsche racing coupé alongside the author's 356A coupé, before it went off on a shopping expedition (author).

ideas, for the 911 series was under development and their engineering principles did not allow them to produce a half-way production car. It had to be either an out-and-out competition car or a totally civilized production car for customers world-wide. It would have been difficult to productionize the 904 as regards noise levels, interior heating and cooling, rattle-free doors, dust-proofing and so on. While a few customers like myself would have foregone all those things for the sheer fun of driving a 904 as a road car, there would not have been enough of us to justify a production line at Zuffenhausen. A pity.

The factory did enter a 904 in the 1965 Monte Carlo Rally, driven by Eugen Bohringer and Rolf Wutherich. They finished an heroic second overall amid snow and ice. Some years afterwards, I was staying at Bohringer's hotel, which overlooks the Daimler-Benz factory in Unterturkheim, high up in the hills where the best German red wine comes from. On the wall of the restaurant is a photograph of that Monte Carlo 904 and when I remarked on it Bohringer chuckled and reminisced about the event. His lasting impression was of the coldness in the cockpit in mid-winter, for the heating system was negligible, and with the air-cooled engine behind him and no water radiator at the front he had virtually no protection from

Of the Porsche kind

the cold. It was only a continual supply of brandy that kept him and his co-driver from freezing to death. He reckoned it was a riot of fun and something nice to have done, but 'never again'.

The 904 was the last serious use of Dr Fuhrmann's 4-camshaft Carrera engine, as the new generation flat-6-cylinder engine was now under way. I had seen some air-cooled cylinder heads with three combustion chambers in the experimental department some time before, and when I had enquired about them I was discreetly told that it was 'something experimental we are doing for General Motors'. Of course, it was the beginning of the 911 era, that air-cooled flat-6 engine carrying Porsche forward until the advent of the water-cooled V8 engine for the 928 and the 4-cylinder in-line engine for the 944. The 904 had a short life, for the new 6-cylinder engine was to appear in its successor, the 906, which really started the upward trend of Porsche sports/racing cars towards total domination of the racing scene, while the

The Porsche 904 GTS went into limited production for purely racing purposes as shown in this photograph, taken at the Zuffenhausen factory. It was a pity that it did not develop into a road going GT car, but Porsche Engineering had bigger and better ideas (Porsche Archives).

production 6-cylinder series 911 model took them to the ultimate heights of the 3.3-litre turbocharged 911.

Looking back, it seems significant that we used Dickie Stoop's 904 to go shopping for a cream cake, for this was the last pure racing, low-volume-production Porsche competition car that you could use as a shopping car.

By the mid-1960s, sports/racing cars had become so specialized and sophisticated that it was no longer possible to drive them on the normal roads. The only place to experience them was a racing circuit or test-track. This naturally took a lot of the fun out of motoring life, but it also opened up a whole new world of experience, even though the opportunities were less frequent. Today's sports/racing cars have such performance and potential that there is not room on the public roads to unleash it. Though a normal being might conduct one around a circuit, it is unlikely that he would be capable of exploiting the full potential of the vehicle. It is just the same with aircraft: whereas you or I could probably manage to get a Tiger Moth or an Auster off the ground after a few minutes' instruction, we would not know how to deal with a Lear Jet or a Falcon 50 without a week of instruction, and

The author climbing out of a Ford GT40 at Goodwood, after trying to drive it himself for a few laps. It was much more satisfying to be taken round in the passenger seat, driven by Sir John Whitmore, who could push the car up to and beyond its limits.

Of the Porsche kind

even then officialdom would call for all manner of licences and qualifications before we could zoom about the sky in one.

The Porsche twin-turbocharged 935GT coupé is a typical modern example. Few people are offered the chance to drive one round a circuit, though the racing teams are often prepared to let you experience one as a passenger to one of the professional drivers. Personally, I would much rather be driven round a circuit by an experienced factory racing driver than try to drive a present-day racing car myself. If I was capable of exploiting a front-line competition car to its full potential round a circuit, I would not be a writer: I'd be a professional racing driver and this book would not be written. It is far better to be given a practical demonstration by a professional than to make a mediocre attempt yourself. Not everyone agrees with this philosophy and many writers and journalists insist on trying to drive racing cars that are beyond their capabilities, never taking the opportunity to experience the potential to its fullest in the capable hands of a known racing driver.

This really came home to me on a test day with a Ford GT40 coupé, when we had all been allowed an opportunity to teeter round a circuit as best we could. I was very conscious that I had not exceeded more than about one-third of the possibilities of the car, apart from straight-line acceleration, which any fool can do. Other journalists were prattling on about how they had 'got the tail out' or 'reached terminal understeer', though I had not noticed them doing it. John Whitmore was standing by at the time. He had raced Ford GT40s and was known for his driving ability, so I said, 'Come on, John, take me for a few laps. I want to find out how good this car is.' This he did willingly, for he loved fast driving, and he flung that car around the circuit right up to and over its limits of cornering and braking. It was terrific and I really enjoyed it. I also learnt so much more about the car. Much later I had a similar opportunity with the Ferrari Berlinetta Boxer, when I got Niki Lauda to take me for some laps, rather than trying to drive it myself.

In the realms of Porsche, this opportunity came one day at Silverstone when Porsche Cars (GB) Ltd arranged a test day for the Press before the BRDC Six Hour Race. Jochen Mass was on hand with a twin-turbo 935 GT coupé. A group of us were standing chatting while Jochen was going round the circuit, warming the car up and generally seeing that all was well. He came into the pit lane with this wild-looking projectile and stopped, and none of us was quite sure what the form was. As I had only just arrived, I assumed that the others had already booked their rides, so I waited for someone to go first. Nobody moved and then Jochen shouted, 'Denis, come.' That was it: I was in the passenger seat and we were off down the pit lane in a shattering

A Passion for Porsches

burst of acceleration and out on to the circuit, while the others were still wondering how their crash-hat buckles fastened.

Once you realize how good the modern competition car is and appreciate that it can generate high G-forces with complete stability, such a ride is not all that exciting; exhilarating, yes, especially the high-speed acceleration such as when you come out of Becketts Corner, through Chapel and down Hanger Straight. Braking on the modern competition car is also something that is difficult to believe. With the incredible adhesion of modern racing tyres, brakes can really be used effectively and the lateness of braking for a corner practised by today's racing driver is something that has to be experienced. Cornering G-forces are no real surprise if you have a feel for tyre adhesion and the cornering power of wide tyres and sophisticated suspension systems.

The modern Porsche 935 with turbocharged 2.8-litre engine could be tuned to develop nearly 600bhp with a top speed of over 200mph, so it is not surprising that the factory no longer let motoring writers out on the road with such cars. The only opportunity to experience them is to be driven by a factory driver (Porsche Archives).

Of the Porsche kind

The solid feel and sound of a well tuned racing engine is always satisfying, for it is in a different world to a normal engine, even to good sports car engines. While I eschew the use of seat belts for normal everyday motoring, I have no compunction about strapping myself firmly to the seat of a modern sports/racing car: not from a safety angle, for I am a fatalist as regards accidents, but purely to stay at one with the car, for the forces generated these days are far more than normal muscular control can cope with. Sideways G-forces under cornering can be controlled by a well fitting seat, but fore and aft G-forces on braking and accelerating are more than you can control. A full harness to strap you firmly down to the seat is all-important.

After the third of my four laps in the 935 with Jochen Mass, the rain started to come down. The final lap on a wet surface was interesting, but gentle by comparison. From then on the 'demonstrations' were a bit more exciting but nothing like so interesting. I was glad I had not hesitated, for the rain persisted for the rest of the morning. With due respect to Jochen Mass, a good healthy racing driver, he is not in the category of the élite. Some of my younger colleagues had been very impressed with the day's experiences, as it was their first ride in such a car, but I was forced to remind them that Jochen was only an average-good racing driver in the upper echelon. I asked them if they could imagine what it would have been like with Pironi or Piquet. They couldn't.

Chapter TWELVE

Owner's troubles

During the course of covering something like half a million miles in Porsche cars, one is bound to meet trouble along the way. Some of the troubles were trivial, some hilarious and others serious. I had various troubles of my own, though fortunately none of them were terminal, and I had trouble with friend's cars, while they had their fair share themselves, some of which I was involved with.

On one visit to the Porsche factory, I called in at the repair shop to see my friend Hubert, who was in charge. There on one of the repair jigs, I saw Steve Wilder's black coupé, looking very battered and second-hand. It had obviously been on its roof in the classic 356 'loop the loop' manoeuvre, but a close look at the damage suggested that he probably got away fairly lightly. 'Herr Wilder has a big accident,' said Hubert, 'he is in the cafe across from the station.' I went back into town and found Steve having a meal. 'So what happened?' was my first question, for he was obviously completely unscathed. 'You know the long straight road out of Swindon towards Cirencester, with the lovely plunge down the hill at Blunsden?' 'Yes', I said. 'And at the top there is a big signboard that says "Accident Black Spot – 27 accidents have taken place here" . . .' 'Well, go on', I said. 'Gee, I guess the council guy is changing it to 28 right now', said Steve with a grin. He was bombing over the brow and down the hill when a car in front of him turned right without signalling. He didn't hit the other car, but the avoiding action he took put the Porsche into the most diabolical series of weaves which eventually ended up with the rear wheels tucking under, while the next lurch flicked it on to its roof and into the hedge. Although the bodywork was battered all over, Steve

The author 'banging on' to the troops after a few laps round Silverstone with Jochen Mass in a 935 turbocharged Porsche. The 'troops' awaiting their turn are, left to right, Peter Windsor (Autocar) Maurice Hamilton (Guardian) and Nigel Roebuck (Autosport) (unknown).

The author's 199-cc Tiger Cub motorcycle on which he nearly repeated the Steve Wilder accident on the famous Blunsden Hill near Swindon.

rattled about inside quite unhurt, apart from the odd bruise. On reflection he wondered if it would have been better to have rammed the other car amidships, for that way at least the culprit would have had some damage to repair; as it was, he got away scot-free.

Luckily the Porsche had not hit any solid objects in its wayward flight and had made a soft landing in the hedge. Once back on its wheels it was still driveable, and Steve had taken it back to Stuttgart for major repairs. About 10 years later I was on that same road, flat-out on my little 199-cc Tiger Cub motorcycle. As I breasted the hill and looked down into the vale towards Cricklade and Cirencester, the road ahead was completely clear except for a Vauxhall Wyvern ahead of me and going my way. 'Wheeee!' I said to myself and kept the throttle up against the stop, crouching down over the tank in the hope of gaining a few more miles per hour. The little Triumph was not very fast but it would wind up and up given a steep hill, and this was one. I had reached about 72mph and all was well with the world, when the Vauxhall began to turn right without any warning, right across my bows. I hadn't a hope of stopping and was completely on the wrong line to go to the left of it. Keeping the throttle against the stop, I flattened myself on the tank and headed over to the right of the road, which luckily was still completely clear. I shot across the front of the Vauxhall at about 75mph, missing it by about a foot and having about the same between me and the edge of the road. As I recovered my composure and went back to the left side of the road, I thought, 'I see what Steve Wilder meant about Blunsden hill.'

On the Porsche 356, the clutch was way down at the back of the car while the clutch pedal was near the front suspension, the connection being by means of a simple open steel cable. In something like 350,000 miles in my own car I never had a cable break on me, though I renewed it occasionally, but on two occasions I was with friends whose cars suffered a breakage. The first occasion was on a trip to Sicily to see the Targa Florio. I had stopped off in Modena and joined Peter Coltrin in his black 356B coupé for the journey south. He was driving down the southern end of the Adriatic coast of Italy, heading for the ferry at Villa S Giovanni to cross the Straights of Messina to the racing island. We were well south of Catanzaro when there was a snap as Pete changed gear and the clutch pedal went down to the floor. We stopped, and sure enough found that the cable had broken where it went into the steel eye that pivoted on the pedal. The nearest point of civilization was Reggio Calabria so I was all for pressing on without the clutch and looking for a helpful garage when we got there. As Pete was unconversant with clutchless driving, I agreed to take over.

Years of vintage motoring had taught me about changing gear without using the clutch and also the tricks of restarting by the use of gravity. That is

Owner's troubles

The author with Peter Coltrin's black 356B after a lunch stop en route for Sicily. Little did they realize that the clutch cable was within hours of breaking (Peter Coltrin).

something you learn very quickly with old cars when the starter motor packs up. With a good vintage 'crash' box, changing gear without using the clutch is no problem. As on a good motor cycle gearbox, it is as easy without as with. The thought of driving the Porsche without the clutch did not worry me in the slightest, but to Pete it was a whole new world. The Porsche started easily on the level when put in gear and driven off on the starter motor until the engine fired. When you are in this predicament, it is surprising how easy it is to find a small slope if you have to stop; then it is even easier to get it rolling on the starter motor in bottom gear. Changing gear on the Porsche baulk-ring syncromesh gearbox is a bit tricky, when compared with the original VW/Porsche 'crash' gearbox used on the early cars. It is still quite practicable, however, and we succeeded in making our way round the toe of Italy and up to Reggio Calabria where we stopped for the night.

Next morning we found a friendly Fiat garage, where an innovative mechanic adapted a Fiat 600 clutch cable to the Porsche, and we continued on our way to Palermo. That temporary repair lasted throughout our visit to

A Passion for Porsches

Sicily and all the way back to Modena, though we took the precaution of getting the Italian mechanic to modify a second Fiat cable as a spare. Back at Bologna, Pete had a proper Porsche cable fitted by the Porsche agents and all was well.

At the end of one racing season, I was travelling to Paris for the Motor Show with Jesse Alexander in his silver 356B coupé. We were bowling merrily along near Nancy, in the days before the autoroutes, when he suffered the dreaded snap and no clutch operation. Once again I took over a clutchless Porsche, as like Pete, Jesse had never driven old cars. I drove it into Nancy where we located a Porsche agent who fitted a new cable while we waited, and Jesse was able to continue driving to Paris.

It always struck me as odd that two of my American friends broke their clutch cables, while I never did in all the Porsche miles I covered. I can only put it down to the fact that I have a sensitive feel for clutches and their mechanisms, due to growing up on motorcycles. They probably used the full travel of the clutch pedal all the time, without realizing it, thus straining the cable to its fullest extent. In addition, as I always did my own servicing, the cable and pivots were kept well lubricated, while the Swiss and Italian local garages that did their servicing for them probably did not appreciate the need for adequate lubrication.

After the 1958 Six Hours Relay Race, our Porsche team went to a restaurant in Aylesbury for a convivial evening with much Porsche talk, where Steve and I regaled everyone with Porsche motoring legends and experiences. Something we had both experienced was the simple fact that a Porsche 356 coupé did not put up much of a bow wave of air ahead of it, having a very smooth nose, with no bluff radiator or opening at the front. Although this helped considerably with the low drag coefficient of the coupé body, it had a side effect in that when travelling at speed, you often hit small birds much more frequently than in a normal car. In a car with a large radiator at the front and a lot of air disturbance, you could literally see small birds using the disturbed air to get more lift, as they would zoom up over the roof if came upon them suddenly. With the Porsche 356 you would often see a bird was suffering from a lack of lift, which meant that if you did not hit it with the nose of the car, then the top of the windscreen and the roof would probably strike it. This was all very unfortunate for the bird population but there was little you could do about it. It was Jean Bugatti who said, many years ago, 'Never swerve for a dog when travelling at high speed. A pedestrian or another vehicle, yes, but a dog, no.' Much as I like birds, you have to be realistic about high-speed motoring.

Ian Scott-Watson and Jimmy Clark were in the group and they listened to our stories with a certain amount of scepticism, though they did agree with us

Owner's troubles

Jesse Alexander's 356B parked behind the author's car at a petrol stop in Switzerland. It was this car that broke its clutch cable on the way to Paris (author).

on those concerning handling. Jimmy in particular was most interested to discuss cornering and balance, tyre treads and widths, weight distribution and so on. When we parted company, Ian and Jimmy got into the white 1600S and headed off up to Scotland, while the rest of us journeyed south to Hampshire.

The following week I received a letter from Ian, saying that they had not really believed our theory about birds and the lack of lift afforded by the front of a Porsche, but that they had now changed their minds. A blackbird had come right through the windscreen, luckily without hurting either of them, but they saw quite clearly that a car with a bluff front and a bow-wave of disturbed air might just have given the bird that extra bit of lift to have cleared the top of the car.

The air flow on those 356 coupés was remarkably good, which considerably

A Passion for Porsches

The 1600S Porsche raced by Jim Clark in the 1958 Silverstone Six Hour Relay Race. On the journey back to Scotland a blackbird went through the windscreen (author).

Owner's troubles

The front of the Porsche 356 was very smooth and devoid of any opening for radiator or cooling air, which gave it very good airflow characteristics over the front and allowed a relatively high maximum speed with comparatively small horsepower output.

improved economical running and their ability to pull a high top gear. One day, an aerodynamicist friend of mine did some air flow tests with me at a sustained 70mph. He had a pretty good idea about what the air *should* be doing over the front of the car and around the windscreen, but as he read his gauges from the pitot head mounted on various parts of the car, he kept saying to himself, 'Cor!' He was very impressed. We had a good example of the air flow over the rear of the car, across the back window, quite accidentally. My friend Sandy Burnett was the third member on a trip and had folded himself up into the space behind the seats, sitting sideways with one eyeball a few inches from the rear window. After a while, he said, 'You won't believe this, but there is a fly on the outside of the rear window and the airflow hasn't blown it off.' We were cruising along at about 50–60mph, so I said, 'Tell me when it gets blown off.' I accelerated gently up to 70, 80 and close on 90mph, and Sandy reported that it was still there, although its legs were bent at the knees. We didn't believe this, but he assured us it was so, because the fly was only about 3 inches from his left eye. I gently slowed down to 45–50mph, whereupon he reported that the fly was still there and had straightened its legs. We thought he was having us on, so I repeated the speed. Sure enough, as we got upwards towards 80mph, the fly's wings and legs were bent down by the down-force of the air-flow, but it was still firmly attached to the glass. With such a close-up view, Sandy was fascinated by the whole thing and we went through the motion once more with the same result. Eventually we slowed right down to below 30mph and suddenly, without warning, the fly was gone. It must have been a very strange sensation for it.

One of the most unbelievable of accidents happened to Peter Coltrin's black 356B when he wasn't in it. We were all staying with Jesse Alexander in his house in the mountains and I thought I would take the opportunity to get my car greased properly and have the oil changed at the same time. I arranged to take it down to the local garage in Meiringen, which was about a vertical mile away, down in the valley, and about 10 miles by way of the mountain pass. Pete was a great one for keeping his car washed and polished, in direct contrast to me, for I cleaned mine about once a year, so he said he'd take his car down as well. Jesse agreed to accompany us in his Borgward estate and bring us back. This we did, returning to Hohfluh to sit in the mountain sunshine, talk motor racing and Porsche motoring, and admire the view over the Alps.

Our peace was disturbed by the ringing of the telephone. Jesse answered it, to return looking more worried than usual. 'Pete,' he murmured, 'there's been an accident.' Pete looked up from his gin and tonic and said, 'So what?' When Jesse replied, 'Your car has been involved', we both sat up and took notice. The phone call had been from the garage owner, who had said, 'You had better come down, there has been an accident.' Jesse had been unable to make him enlarge on this bald statement: 'All the guy would say was *unfall* – accident. We'd better go down.' As we drove back down the mountain pass in the Borgward, we were very puzzled. We could not see how Pete's Porsche could be involved in an accident since he had parked it on the wash area himself. We wondered if it was my car that had been shunted, while out on test after the oil change, but Jesse said that the garage owner had mentioned it was the black Porsche, and mine was blue. We thought of everything: they had washed Pete's car with the windows open and it was full of water; they had put it up on the hydraulic hoist and crushed it into the

Owner's troubles

garage roof; they had jacked it up on one side to clean the wheels and it had fallen off the jack on to the garage boy's leg; a big truck had swept into the forecourt and smashed into the Porsche, and so on and so on. At least it kept our minds busy while we drove down to Meiringen, totally bewildered and intrigued to see what had happened.

When we got to the garage, there was Pete's once immaculate Porsche coupé, battered and bent and covered in mud. It had obviously been end over end, side over side, and back on to its wheels again in the most monumental private accident, for there were no signs of contact with another car or any solid object. Every panel was dented, including the roof. It turned out that the young lad who had been washing and polishing it had finished the job quickly. As he had never driven a Porsche, he thought he would have a quick trip up the road in it. It was a bit wet and greasy down in the valley and he was hardly out of sight of the garage before he lost control and looped-the-loop over a ditch and into a field. Apart from being shaken up, he was unscathed and had returned on foot to report to the 'boss', who had not known he had gone off in the car. He was sacked from his job even before the garage proprietor had phoned Jesse, which was about the only consolation Pete got.

As we drove back to Hohfluh, Pete said, 'I'm glad I didn't ask for a full service.' Pete was always philosophical about things like that. Eventually, the garage man's trade insurance paid for a total rebuild, but what irked Pete was that the ensuing investigation by the local police revealed that one of the rear tyres was a bit worn. He was accordingly fined for having a car on Swiss roads in an unsafe condition.

Jack Burke phoned me one day to say that his Carrera engine was making an ominous ticking noise and he had arranged for a complete engine overhaul back at the factory. He wanted to know if I would be prepared to drive it to Stuttgart for him. I went to see him and after listening carefully to the noise we were both pretty sure it was a roller bearing breaking up in the crankshaft. Although I had my doubts about continuing to run the engine, he was prepared to take a chance. After all, if it was going to have a new crank and rods anyway, it didn't much matter if I ruined the existing one by driving it the 600 miles to Stuttgart. With fingers crossed and clutch foot at the ready, I set off. After getting from Hampshire to Dover without the noise becoming any worse, I gained a bit of confidence. I pussy-footed across France by minor roads, rather than taking the Belgian route and the German Autobahn where it would have been difficult not to go fast. I felt there was less incentive to go fast on the French roads, and that if anything did break I would have an easier time being retrieved from a French road than from an Autobahn. I crossed the Rhine at Rastatt and then decided to use the Autobahn for the last leg of the journey from Pforzheim to Stuttgart, as the normal German roads were not very good and were very slow.

About 30 miles from Stuttgart, I was cruising quietly along on the minimum of throttle opening, feeling that all was well and that I was going to make Zuffenhausen safely. There was a sudden 'clonk' and the engine locked up solid without any warning. I declutched and coasted to a stop on the side of the Autobahn. My investigation revealed no awful holes in the engine nor pools of oil underneath, but the engine simply would not turn. The only thing to do was to cry for help. Across the fields I could see a small village, so leaving the Carrera locked up with a note on the windscreen, I climbed over the fence and set off across the fields to the houses.

Now my command of the German language was not terribly good, but somehow I managed to communicate to the countryfolk in one of the houses that I needed to use their telephone. At the Porsche factory I had a very good friend in Dr Hortolf Biesenberger, who worked in the press and public relations department. He was, and still is, a devoted Porsche enthusiast and ran a Cabriolet 356 which had been one of the factory supported cars in the Liège-Rome-Liège Rally some years before. He now used it for everyday transport, powered by the current 1,600-cc engine. Like me, Hortolf spent a lot of time going to races and his Cabriolet was as famous in the paddocks of Europe as my light blue coupé. It was early evening, warm and sunny, and luckily he was still in his office. 'Wait by the car,' he told me, 'I'll be with you.' I went back across the fields to the stricken Carrera and, sure enough, it was not long before I saw the dark grey Cabriolet coming into view on the other side of the Autobahn. With a wave Hortolf went by, for of course he had to go way past me to the next turn-off before he could leave the west-bound side and return along the east-bound side. Eventually he arrived, and after hitching a rope to the Carrera, he towed me to Zuffenhausen and then took me to my hotel.

What was quite remarkable was that while I was waiting for Dr Biesenberger, and throughout the tow, we never saw a sign of the Autobahn Polizei. In those far off days, traffic density even on the Mannheim–Munich Autobahn was pretty sparse, especially early on a weekday evening in 1958. While writing this book in 1982, I met Hortolf at the Monaco Grand Prix, for we are both still in motor racing, though he left the Porsche firm many years ago to set up on his own in publicity, journalism and photography. We reminisced about that evening, laughing at the possibility of repeating it today. The Autobahns are now so full of traffic that to attempt a tow with a slack rope would be a nightmare, and it is unlikely that you would get far before the Polizei and the ADAC Rescue Service arrived, with lights flashing in all directions, plastic cones everywhere, and a 10-mile build-up of traffic

The author's 356A in its final form, by which time it had become something of a 'special' with Carrera suspension bits, a 1600S engine, different steering and different wheels from standard, as well as body trim alterations (author).

The author also had his troubles. Here is his 356A after being rammed by an Austin A40 while he was stationary. Even in this state it was still driveable but needed a major rebuild (author).

jams as people slowed down to ogle at a car being lifted on to a transporter. I have known slow-down chain-reaction on the Autobahns to build up to a stationary jam 10 or even 20 miles before a tiny accident. The sea of blue and orange flashing lights of the Polizei and the Hilfservice seems to mesmerize the travelling public into a 5mph crawl. In 1958, we just hitched on the rope and rejoined the Autobahn at 60–70mph without disturbing anyone.

Hortolf Biesenberger is a remarkable man, for he lost his right arm a long time ago in an accident, yet he can do as much, if not more than most people with two arms. The speed of his gear changes on his Porsches was outstanding: he would steady the steering wheel with his thigh and reach across with his left arm to the gear lever, his Cabriolet and the three subsequent Porsches he owned being left-hand drive. To see him extract a cigarette from his cigarette case and light it, all with one hand, is to understand the meaning of dexterity.

Chapter THIRTEEN

A New Generation

By the early 1960s, it was pretty obvious that the Porsche 356 series was reaching the end of its development, for it had been in production for more than 10 years. From the simple Volkswagen based coupé of 1950, it had evolved through the 356A and 356B, which were the peak years of the original conception, to the 356C and SC, the Super 75 and the Super 90. The 1,500-cc and 1,600-cc Carrera offshoots had made the limitations of the original design even more obvious, but I don't think anyone outside the factory could really see what the next step would be. That the basic 'beetle' Porsche had been a success was undeniable, and for a car to retain its original shape for 10 years was surely proof that it was right to begin with.

Naturally, there were all sorts of rumours and stories going the rounds in Stuttgart and in the sporting world, and even when some of us noticed air-cooled cylinder heads with three combustion chambers we were not too sure, for the party-line to those of us who were nosey was that Porsche were doing some experimental work for an outside firm. This was true enough and what we saw was more than likely work for General Motors for the Chevrolet Corvair, but it was no coincidence that Porsche thinking was along the same lines – of a horizontally opposed flat-6-cylinder engine in two banks of three cylinders.

Eventually, the all-new Porsche 2-litre 901 appeared. While it followed many of the original Porsche ideas, such as an air-cooled flat engine mounted behind the rear axle and Porsche baulk-ring synchromesh gearbox, independent suspension to all four wheels and a smooth coupé body, it was totally new. It was an altogether larger car, with two small seats behind the driver and passenger, more luggage room in the front, and longer in the wheelbase, and as first seen it seemed a very big car for a 2-litre engine to propel. At the time I doubt whether anyone visualized the engine growing to a turbocharged 3.3 litres, without taking up any more space or calling for a bigger car.

Although the original announcement said that the new model would be called the 901, it was not long before it was renamed the 911, usually referred to as the 'nine eleven'. At the time there was a story going the rounds that the Peugeot company had taken out a patent to restrict model numbers with a zero in the middle to themselves exclusively. Due to this, Porsche had to agree to change their number. When it was mentioned that BMW had been using 501, 502, 503 and 507, and Bristol had been using 400, 401, 402, 403, 404 and 405, the story went that Peugeot considered them to be small specialist manufacturers, while they considered Porsche to be a large manufacturer, which was a nice compliment to the Zuffenhausen firm. With Ferrari later producing the 206, the 308 and 400, and Daimler-Benz the 200, 300 and 600, the Peugeot story falls a bit flat, but it was nice at the time, and Porsche certainly changed the number of the new car from 901 to 911, even though all the original brochures and publicity material had been issued for the 901.

While at the factory one day in 1964, I was offered a test run in one of the early prototype cars. Without hesitation, I took off for the Solitude circuit and the countryside south of the Autobahn. Although this entirely new Porsche design had a lot of good points and was very interesting, I did not take to it. Compared to the 356 series cars, it seemed huge, and while the flat-6 engine was quite pleasant, it was pretty noisy without the excitement of the noisy 2-litre Carrera engine. It was certainly a better engine than the pushrod 4-cylinder, which it should have been, being 400cc larger, but my feeling was that Porsche had taken two steps forward and three backwards. The bigger and better engine seemed necessary only to propel a bigger and presumably better car. Instead of looking at it as the beginning of a new era, there was a tendency to view it as another step in the development of the 356, which was totally wrong. What one should have done was to compare it with the 356 of 1950 and then add 10 years of development.

While it went along quite smoothly and rode well on its new suspension, it rolled very badly on hard cornering, and even on not so hard cornering for that matter. With good anti-roll bars, competition shock absorbers and attention to tyres, the 356 cornered with remarkably little roll, keeping a very flat and even keel no matter how hard you cornered. This new model seemed to roll on to its door handles at the very sight of a corner, by comparison, and seemed more like an Opel than a Porsche. I did not like the

A New Generation

handling at all, and compared to a 2-litre Carrera the engine seemed gutless.

I still had my well-developed 356A at this time and I was desperately looking for something to replace it. I had hoped that the 911 would be the answer. Having got used to the mechanical simplicity of the 356A, I was reluctant to take on the much more complex 911, especially as I did not really like the car and its aesthetics did nothing for me. Consequently, I said goodbye to my Porsche and took up E-type Jaguar motoring, though I did not join the Jaguar family in the same way I had joined the Porsche family.

Although I no longer spent all my time driving in a Porsche, I did not leave the family completely, for Porsche were still very active in racing and racing was still my main sphere of activity. In consequence I kept in very close touch with the world of Porsche and took every opportunity to drive all the developments of the 911 as they came along. By now Porsche production had expanded beyond all recognition and the days of the factory knowing all their customers by name were long gone. They were now producing a much more

The new generation of Porsche cars presented an altogether much sleeker and more purposeful-looking image, even though it followed the concepts of the 356 with the engine behind the rear wheels (author).

A Passion for Porsches

The 911 Porsche was one of those cars that invited you to drive it. The Reutter reclining seat, the angle of the steering wheel, the instruments arrayed before the driver in an arc, and the central rpm indicator were all conducive to 'driving in its purest form' (author).

When the new 6-cylinder Porsche first appeared it was designated the 901. The caption on the back of this rare photograph states, 'The new Porsche Type 901: 2 litre, six-cylinder, two o.h.c.' All the publicity and advertising material had to be changed to read 911 after Peugeot complained (Porsche Archives).

sophisticated car that was not aimed solely at the sporting world, so not unnaturally various rather 'ordinary' facets crept into the development of the 911. One of these was a contraption called the 'Sportomatic', which made the use of the clutch unnecessary.

In less than two years, the 911 was developed into a much more acceptable motorcar, and when I got the chance to do a 1,200-mile road test for *Motor Sport* at the beginning of 1966, I raved about the 911/2000, as it was known. All the rolling about on corners had been eliminated, the ride was greatly improved by attention to shock-absorbers and spring rates, and the engine gave 130 (DIN) horsepower, all of which put the car into the place that was originally intended for it, namely as a follow-on to the 2-litre 4-cylinder Carrera 356.

Like all Porsches, it enjoyed being driven on the rev-counter and the higher the rpm the happier the engine seemed, while in true Porsche fashion the top gear ratio was such that you could not possibly over-rev in top gear. In the lower gears you needed to watch the rev-counter, for though peak power came at 6,100rpm, the engine would go singing on up to 6,500 or 6,800 with less fuss than it made at 5,000. To encourage this habit of driving

A Passion for Porsches

Ten years of development saw the 911 turn into one of the world's greatest performance cars in the shape of a 3-litre turbocharged model, which still retained the basic shape of the original design (Porsche Archives).

Termed the 911L and outwardly a normal 911, it was not until you started to drive that you discovered the joys, or horrors, of the 'Sportomatic' transmission. When driven above the range of the 'Sportomatic' gizmoes, the car was a good, honest 911 (author).

A New Generation

The author's 4.2-litre E-type Jaguar coupé which he used as a yardstick against which to measure the performance of other cars, including 911 Porsches during the 1960s.

on the rev-counter, the large, clearly marked instrument was mounted right in front of the driver, the new two-pronged steering wheel allowing a clear view at all times. Some engines will let you know when they are approaching their maximum rpm, either by becoming noisy or by feeling rough, but a Porsche engine, like a Ferrari engine, enjoys high rpm and sings away merrily the harder you drive it. While 6,800rpm was the recommended maximum, it was all too easy to exceed this if you did not pay attention, for at that speed the engine sounded like a dynamo, and felt like one. In fifth gear it would pull 6,200rpm very easily, and given a reasonable length of motorway, it would build up to 6,400rpm, which was about 130mph. This was good going for a 2-litre car, but I had done a lot of Jaguar motoring by this time, and by comparison I felt the 911 lacked absolute power for a car of its size. There was no doubt that if you rowed it along with the gear-lever, it could be made to go, but the effortless performance of 4.2 litres of Jaguar E-type had spoilt me.

A Passion for Porsches

Variety is the spice of motoring, as shown by this photograph of the 911L in between an E-type Jaguar from Britain and a Mazda with Wankel rotary engine from Japan. Note the height and frontal area of the Porsche relative to that of the Jaguar (author).

It is said that 'power corrupts, and absolute power corrupts absolutely', and that is certainly true as far as engines are concerned. I had been happily corrupted by the absolute power of the E-type – not only by its horsepower, but by the enormous torque it developed. My simple estimation of this was to cruise at 100mph with everything steady, and then push the accelerator pedal right down to the floor. In the E-type the long nose rose as the tail squatted down under the acceleration, and the surge forwards to 110, 120, 125mph was one of the most satisfying things in motoring. On the 911 this was missing, for all it did was to make more noise with no noticeable surge forwards.

The reason for this personal test procedure was that I was spending a lot of time cruising at 100-105mph, a leisurely gait for an E-type, and that instant surge forwards was essential to my personal well-being. I have never believed

A New Generation

believed in using brakes unless absolutely necessary, and in fast motoring I found that if you looked well ahead and used your anticipatory senses, you could avoid impending trouble by accelerating rather than by trying to stop, especially when motoring on Autobahnen and Autostrade. That instant surge to 125mph, to overtake something that was going to impede your path, made for much smoother journeys. In the 911, to get that surge of acceleration would have meant snicking down into fourth gear, and by that time it could be too late. Even if it wasn't, the change down and then back up again would upset the rhythm of a journey, even though the Porsche gearbox is just about the best ever made. In short journeys, dashing about from A to B and across to C, this was not important, but when one was putting 600 miles into a day, and repeating it on the second and third day, rhythm became crucial.

In concluding the test of the first fully sorted out 911, I rated it very highly, but made the remark that if Dr Porsche and his men could find a way of getting the power and torque of a 4.2-litre Jaguar engine into the 911, they would have the perfect GT car. This was in 1966 and little did I realize that 10 years later they would achieve exactly that, and a bit more for luck, with the 3-litre turbocharged car.

Without a doubt, if I had been living in Switzerland and continuously making journeys over the Alps and down to the south of Italy, through Calabria, a 911 would have been the ultimate car, but for certain other uses it bore no comparison to a Jaguar. On tick-over, the flat-6 engine rattled and clanked like a bucket full of nails being shaken about. Although it all went smooth and quiet at a touch of the accelerator, it did mean that it was a bit anti-social when manoeuvring about in a confined space late at night. The E-type was elegance personified under such circumstances, for you could leave it at 600rpm on tick-over with not a sound coming from the engine or the exhaust, and shuffle to and fro without touching the accelerator pedal, easing the great car about like a large boat in a harbour. The 911 had to be revved above tick-over before the clutch bit, and the clanking and whirring seemed loud enough to wake the whole neighbourhood. But then the 911 was not really intended for that sort of thing: it was built for motoring and motoring hard, and when used as intended it really came into its own. The harder you drove it the happier it seemed, and it always seemed to stay with you no matter how much you provoked it. I have known people who have spun a 911 Porsche into a ditch, but I have never understood how they managed it. Again, as with the old 356A, some people put them on their roofs, but I never did, although I did just about every trick in the 356 book apart from that.

That the Porsche firm was moving into a new world of ownership was also

A Passion for Porsches

evidenced by the fuel consumption of the 911. This was around 18mpg at best, whereas the little 356 series would show as much as 34mpg. Even when spending all day in second and third gear through Calabria, the 356 dropped to only 28mpg, while similar motoring in a 911 would have seen it hard pressed to record 16mpg. This was one aspect of Porsche development that came in for a lot of attention. Ultimately, the 911 series became very fuel-efficient and was developed to run on very low-grade petrols quite happily. Another feature of the new generation of Porsche cars was that they were now wholly Porsche, with not a vestige of Volkswagen remaining. Thus, no longer could you get parts at VW prices or get service in any VW garage. This characteristic of the Porsche had been changing over the years. By the time of the SC and Super 90, which took over from the 356B, the Volkswagen lineage had nearly disappeared. With the 911 series it was gone for ever.

The opportunity for me to road-test Porsche cars for *Motor Sport* magazine seemed to arise about every two years, which was a convenient way of keeping in touch with Zuffenhausen developments. Apart from a few sidesteps, the development of the 911 progressed steadily forwards. One side step, already

The size of the mid-engined Lotus Europa is clearly shown by this photograph of the author talking to Huschke von Hanstein, who is in the car. He is hearing about Porsche plans for a much better mid-engined sports car! (Peter Coltrin).

154

A New Generation

mentioned briefly, was the 'Sportomatic' gearbox. By the late 1960s, traffic congestion and chaos in cities was getting out of control, and Porsche thought that their customers would need something in the way of an automatic transmission to ease the chore of traffic driving. Rather than go to a straight-forward automatic three-step transmission, such as they had developed for Daimler-Benz, they chose to keep their splendid gearbox and adapt a sort of automatic clutch to it.

The whole thing was a step side-ways. First of all, the gearbox had only four speeds in it, against the normal five speeds, and between the engine and the gearbox was an hydraulic torque-converter as well as the normal plate clutch. A vacuum-servo mechanism operated the clutch, the servo being energized by an electrical contact on the gear selector mechanism. As you pushed the lever into first gear, for example, the lever did two things. First it triggered off the servo to withdraw the clutch, and then it pushed the gear into engagement. When fully home, the lever actuated another electrical contact which cut out the servo and allowed the clutch to engage, but the torque converter kept everything at rest until the engine speed was increased, whereupon the hydraulic coupling took up the drive and the car moved forwards. At 3,500rpm the torque converter went 'solid' and you had a normal 4-speed Porsche 911, but with no clutch pedal. To change gear, you merely moved the gear lever, the electrical contacts doing the clutch operation for you. Although the car was tolerable if driven in the upper regions of the rev-counter, when the torque-converter did not function, it was not a patch on the normal Porsche 5-speed gearbox. I was not enamoured by 'Sportomatic' and I suspect true Porsche owners were not either, for it died a quiet death after a brief life.

I had borrowed the 'Sportomatic' car from AFN Ltd. They were still looking after Porsche interests in the UK, so much so that they had by now formed a subsidiary company called Porsche Cars Great Britain Ltd, though they were still operating from the famous old Falcon Works in Isleworth where the Frazer Nash cars used to be made. When I returned the car to W. H. (Bill) Aldington, who looked after all the road test and publicity activity for the firm, I had to confess that I was not impressed by it, although it was admittedly an interesting technical exercise. I still felt that the 911 was one of the world's great GT cars, but the 'Sportomatic' did nothing for it.

During the time I had that car on test, I also had the opportunity to try a Mazda coupé powered by a Wankel rotary engine, and, of course, I was also running the E-type Jaguar. It suddenly struck me that the pistons of all three cars were going in all directions. The Porsche pistons were travelling to and fro across the car, in a horizontal plane, the Jaguar pistons were going up and

A Passion for Porsches

Porsche have not made many mistakes during their 34 years as automobile manufacturers, but one that seemed to 'miss the boat' was the 914. Porsches normally have a purposeful look of speed even when stationary, but the casual observer could be forgiven for wondering which way the 914 was supposed to go.

down in line along the centre of the car, and the Mazda pistons were going round and round. Add the variety of the Porsche being air-cooled and each bank of cylinders having a single camshaft to operate the valves, the Jaguar being water cooled and having two overhead camshafts to operate the valves, and the Mazda having neither valves nor camshafts and being very reliant on oil cooling as well as water cooling, and you have an interesting trio of cars. One from Germany, one from Great Britain and one from Japan, and it was difficult to say which was 'the odd man out'.

One thing was clear and that was that no-one was copying Porsche design trends: you could say that Porsche Engineering was forging a lonely path. While the conception of the 911 was everyone's idea of the ideal GT car, most people agreed that if you had to follow the Porsche route, you would be hard pressed to match their design and quality. Porsche Engineering was becoming a by-word for excellence in the automobile world, accepted everywhere as being as near to perfection as was possible, with no short cuts to save money or time.

A New Generation

When the 911 first appeared, Porsche realized they were starting to move into a new market, so as a sort of interim model, perhaps to keep some of the old 356 people happy, they marketed a model called the 912. This was to all intents and purposes a 911 coupé, but instead of being powered by the new flat-6-cylinder 2-litre engine, it was equipped with the last derivative of the Volkswagen pushrod power unit as developed through all the 356 models. As I did not really take to the 911 from the start, I did not even bother to try a 912, but it was probably quite a good model for newcomers to the Porsche family. Naturally, it was not as expensive or complicated as the 911, and it was a lot cheaper to run, especially if you lived in an insurance-conscious country. It did not develop far, as once the 911 was sorted out, it became so popular that there really was no need for the mundane 912.

Another side-step that Porsche made at about this time was the 914. I had gone to the Targa Florio in Sicily in a Lotus Europa, one of the early models which used the Renault 16 engine and gearbox, and I let Huschke von Hanstein try it out. Not unnaturally, he was not very impressed, for those early Lotus cars were a bit primitive and by Porsche standards still had a 'home-made' air about them. The reason why I liked the Europa at the time was because the conception was right for a small GT car, with the engine behind the driver but in front of the rear axle. In contrast, Jaguars were 'vintage' in conception, with a huge engine at the front driving the rear wheels, while Porsches had the engine too far behind the driver, out beyond the rear axle. Although the Lotus Europa was underpowered and a bit primitive, it was a superb little car as far as handling and ride were concerned. I happened to say to Huschke, 'If this was made by Porsche, it would be a terrific little car.' At this, he replied to the effect that I was taking words out of his mouth, unofficially confirming that Porsche were building a true mid-engined car. The 914 turned out to be exactly that but to me it was a disaster.

Ever since the start of Volkswagen in 1938, there have been close ties between VW and Porsche, and business deals between the two companies were always going on. The 914 was the unfortunate result of one of these deals. The idea was that it should be a joint VW-Porsche effort, designed by Porsche and built by them, using Volkswagen components where possible and marketed by Volkswagen. The car was actually called the VW-Porsche 914, but it turned out to be more of a Volkswagen than a Porsche. It was powered by the old flat-4-cylinder pushrod Porsche engine, though a version using the flat-6 Porsche 911 engine was tried. Altogether it was a typical product of the 'swinging sixties' when the pop-world was totally misled into thinking that ugly was beautiful. Whereas the 911 coupé was a sleek and purposeful-looking machine, the 914 was square and slab-sided with bizarre styling. It

A Passion for Porsches

The 914 from some angles reminded me of a frog about to leap, rather than a high-performance car about to drive off. This one was still in use in Munich in 1982 (author).

certainly did nothing to enhance the Porsche image of 'what looks right is right'. In tune with the times, the cockpit was unnecessarily wide without offering any additional advantage, such as a third seat between the driver and passenger, and the driving position was most peculiar. I once sat in one and that was enough: I did not want to know about driving it. When you got into a 911, the seat fitted like a glove, the steering wheel and controls were exactly right, all the instruments were where you wanted them, and the whole car exuded an atmosphere that said, 'Come on, drive me.' In the 914 I felt that the atmosphere was saying, 'Aren't I way out and crazy, man!' Had I mentioned driving it, I felt it would have looked at me and said, 'Ducky, are you mad?'

Chapter
FOURTEEN

The 911 grows up

As we have seen, it took Porsche very little time to eradicate the faults of the original 901 (911) design. Once the factory had been given over entirely to the production of the 6-cylinder 911 models, improvements came thick and fast. In spite of what a lot of people thought, the 4-cylinder VW-based car was dead and buried as far as sales were concerned, and sales are what govern factory policy. The 911 was a winner and a lot of research and development was put into it, closely coupled to an active racing programme for both factory cars and private entrants.

Although the factory racing department was concentrating on an overall victory campaign, totally divorced from production cars, with the 8-cylinder and 12-cylinder racing engines and one-off sports/racing cars, they were still very committed to racing in the Gran Turismo (GT) category with competition versions of the 911. Naturally, customers who wanted to race were given great encouragement, and optional performance equipment was soon available for the 911. Invariably this performance equipment eventually passed into production and became the normal wear for standard cars, while bigger and better things were developed for the competition cars. Like the original 1500 Super and the 4-cam Carrera, the 911 competition model was a car that could be driven from Germany to Sicily, raced in the Targa Florio, and driven back home again. It was not unusual for a club-racing driver to pick up a new 911 from the Stuttgart factory, drive it south over the Alps, through Switzerland, down the whole length of Italy, and across to Sicily, by which time it would be well run in. Then he would practise and compete in the Targa Florio over 10 or 11 laps of the 44-mile mountain circuit, and

A Passion for Porsches

The Porsche 911S was the first step in a forward direction for the series. Note the polished 'spokes' of the alloy wheels on this 1969/70 model and the complete absence of aerodynamic aids (author).

invariably finish in the money. Porsche 911 failures in long-distance racing were few and far between, and he would have every chance of picking up quite good prize money in the GT category. After the race he would drive back to France or England and sell the car at a profit, having had two weeks' holiday and racing for no cost at all.

The first signs of the direction in which development of the 911 was heading was the introduction of an increase in engine size from 2.0 litres to 2.2 litres. It was not such that it made any startling performance changes, but it increased the torque figures and there was more power available in the middle speed ranges. Already there were 4- and 5-speed gearboxes available according to choice, and an S version of the 911 was outstripping the standard version. The biggest advantage of the 2.2-litre engined car was the improved acceleration, especially in the middle speed range. As Porsche publicity pointed out, 'This is especially advantageous where overtaking is concerned – possibly the major problem in today's congested road conditions.' How right they were, and this was 1969. They were talking, of course, about speeds around 60–70mph, but the 'oomph' at 100mph was still

The 911 grows up

not enough to satisfy me. However, the extra torque of the 2.2-litre engine made it a lot more fun to drive, even if you did have to keep an eye on the rev-counter all the time, and stir about in the gearbox continuously in order to get really exciting performance. In true Porsche fashion, top gear was very high, so that the 911S version of the 2.2-litre would wind up to around 140mph on an Autobahn – but it took some time.

Not content with improving the engine, Porsche naturally improved all the other vital parts of the car: the brakes, the shock-absorbers, the steering, the lights, the seats, and so on. The 911 was developing in all directions and it was all contained within the basic bodyshell evolved in 1964. At all times, the 911 driver was confronted by a large, clear rev-counter in the centre of the instrument panel, unobstructed by the steering wheel spokes and with a red line at 7,400rpm. Hard driving in any Porsche was satisfactory, for the flat-6-cylinder engine never showed any signs of distress when taken up to the

The 911 Porsche in 3-litre Carrera RSR form was a 'ready to race' competition car and this one was raced by Nick Faure for AFN Ltd, the Isleworth Porsche concessionaires. The opening under the front bumper was for a large oil cooler as the RSR engine was more oil-cooled than air-cooled.

red line. In fact, it hummed round so smoothly that it encouraged you to use peak rpm just for the joy of it, especially in third and fourth gears.

During the next 10 years, the 911 grew and grew in all directions technically, but always within the basic size and shape of the original car, which really was a remarkable feat of engineering. Many cars grow in terms of performance and technical improvements, but suffer by getting bigger and heavier – a pitfall the 911 avoided. The engine grew to 2.4 litres, then to 2.7 litres, on up to 3.0 litres and finally to 3.3 litres, all the time remaining the same basic air-cooled flat-6-cylinder. As always, lessons learned in racing were passed on to production. If ever a firm personified the saying, 'Racing improves the breed', it is the firm of Dr Ing hc F. Porsche KG. Naturally, I took every opportunity to drive various versions of the 911 whenever possible, as the whole engineering of Porsche cars set standards by which to judge all others, even if out-and-out performance could be bettered.

In 1973 I at last found a Porsche that satisfied my every need. This was the Carrera version of the 2.7 litre. The name Carrera, as has been explained, stemmed from the Carrera Pan-Americana in which Dr Fuhrmann's 4-cam engine performed so well, and became synonymous at Porsche for 'performance'. It was thus carried on into the 911 series. More than that, it was applied to a model that could be used for competition work as well as roadwork, still maintaining the principle started in 1956. At the 1,000 kilometre race on the beautiful Osterreichring in 1972, the Porsche factory ran the first 2.7-litre 911 coupé. It was fitted with various aerodynamic aids to stability at high speed, in the form of an air dam at the front to prevent air getting under the car and lifting it, and a small spoiler across the tail to increase the downforce on the rear wheels. This was a prototype for a run of 500 similar models, marketed under the name Carrera RS (Rennsport). It could be ordered in 'touring' form with all mod cons, radio, carpets and lots of interior trim, or in 'competition' form devoid of trimmings and ready to race.

The Aldington family were still looking after Porsche interests in Great Britain and I was able to borrow their first 2.7-litre Carrera RS – in fact, I did quite a lot of the initial running-in for them. They promised me that once it was fully run in, it would have enough performance to satisfy even my demands. Porsche standards of running-in are very realistic. The instructions were simply 'Don't go over 5,000rpm to start with.' As this was 100mph in fifth gear, the mileage soon built up and I was allowed to increase the engine speed by increments of 500rpm. At 6,000rpm it was beginning to go, and by the time I was able to use 6,500rpm I was becoming more than impressed by the performance. When I was eventually allowed to go to the red-line

The 911 grows up

at 7,200–7,400rpm, this latest offering from Stuttgart was really on its way. As well as the shattering performance, it had everything else in equal quantities. Its braking, steering, road-holding, ride and cornering power were all of an immensely high order, well able to cope with the power output of the engine. When cruising at 110mph in fifth gear, you had only to flatten the accelerator pedal for the car to surge forward to 130mph or more. No longer was it necessary to change down to fourth gear before high-speed acceleration came in, which was just as well for on this model the gear-change pattern had been altered.

Previously, on the 5-speed Porsche gearbox, the top four gear positions were in the standard pattern of an H, while first gear position was a dog-leg back to the left. This meant that, once under way, you could forget first gear and use the four upper gears as fast as you could move the lever. One section of the Porsche-buying public, and it was a large section, seemed unable to cope with this layout, complaining that when changing up from first gear, it was too easy to move too far across the H-gate, into fourth rather than second gear. To appease this strange section of the motoring public, a new gate pattern was brought in, whereby the lower four gear positions formed the H pattern, while fifth was a dog-leg movement over and up to the right. On a left-hand-drive Porsche, which is how the 911 was originally designed, this was not too bad. The push away from you with the right hand flowed quite nicely from fourth to fifth position, for with the Porsche baulk-ring syncromesh mechanism the change was still as rapid as ever. However, on a right-hand-drive car, changing gear from fourth to fifth position with the left hand was not at all pleasant, neither was changing down from fifth to fourth. Anyone who has not tried both left-hand and right-hand-drive Porsches might find this difficult to appreciate, but anyone who has will be well aware of the difference. Fortunately, the performance of the 2.7-litre Carrera RS was such that there was enough 'oomph' at 100mph or more in top gear to make a change down unnecessary, which was just as well. With tyres and suspension improving as rapidly as engine performance, the cornering on the Carrera RS was reaching the point where it was becoming impossible to drive the car to its limits on the open road. Even when driving fast, you always seemed to have a reserve of everything available, which makes a fast car very safe in the right hands.

When I returned the 2.7-litre to Isleworth, I happily admitted that it had more than enough performance by my standards. Unfortunately, it had come too late, for I was already on my second 4.2-litre E-type Jaguar, and Carrera RS motoring was beyond my economical means, with a gaping abyss looming ahead in the form of inflation. At that time, in 1973, a mere 10 years ago, the 2.7-litre Carrera RS cost £6,255, and you could have had that and a family saloon as well for under £10,000 in total. Today, that amount of money buys you only a rather dull Eurobox. Barely a year after the Carrera RS was introduced, the ordinary 'cooking' 911 with 2.7-litre engine was costing £6,249, while the real performance Porsches were soaring away into the realms of fantasy as regards money.

I have said previously that 'Power corrupts . . .' and it has always been that way with me: any Porsche less than a Carrera 2.7 litre was of little interest. Exacerbating my reluctance to accept second-best was the fact that the roads of Europe were becoming very crowded, with rules and regulations springing up everywhere. Even Spain had discovered the double yellow line down the centre of the road, to control traffic and prevent overtaking. Lorries, motor homes, family boxes and cars with caravans on tow were ruling the roads of Europe, effectively preventing any thought of overtaking for mile after mile. The high performance car was being stifled by the over-population of the roads, and the frustration factor was becoming greater than the satisfaction factor. That meant that it was time for a change. Consequently, I put aside all thought of using a Porsche Carrera RS, and instead took to a fast motorcycle as the only way to continue enjoying the roads of Europe.

However, for those who were prepared to suffer the stifling road conditions or confine their driving to motorways, the Porsche factory continued to develop the 911 even further. What was offered for sale was a direct spin-off from racing, for the 911 was still very active in competitions, and on the race-track there are no limits to development. The engine was enlarged to 3.0 litres and turbocharging was applied, all still in the same basic bodyshell, though wider wheels and tyres had demanded bulges over the wheel arches, and aerodynamic spoilers had grown fore and aft. While such things were out of my realm for everyday motoring, I did not miss an opportunity to borrow the latest offerings and in 1977 I experienced a whole new world of Porsche.

This was in the form of a 3.0-litre turbocharged 911, the actual car that had been at the Earls Court Motor Show in 1976, on the stand of Porsche Cars Great Britain Ltd. The turbocharged 911 competition model had swept all before it in GT racing, and, as always, Porsche followed the basic principle that racing success should lead directly to the production line. At the Motor Show the Porsche Turbo, as it became known, was the centrepiece of the stand, painted brilliant white with red, white and blue striping along the side, with the interior done out in a rather bizarre fashion in the same colours. It was all in aid of the image of Martini-Rossi who had been supporting the works Porsche team, and this 'Martini Team Replica' was as much a status symbol as a production car. On the Motor Show stand it stood at £21,162, more than three times the cost of the 2.7-litre Carrera RS a mere three years

The 911 grows up

before! The first reaction of the Porsche sales department, when the factory said they were putting the 3.0-litre turbocharged car into production, was that it was too much of everything and nobody would be able to afford it. Porsche Engineering knew better and the original idea of a limited run of 500 cars had to be amended very quickly to allow for a second run of 500.

The business of turbocharging can be explained most simply as using the exhaust gases from the flat-6-cylinder engine to drive a small turbine which is coupled to an air compressor. This compressor feeds air into the inlet manifold under a pressure regulated by the 'boost control unit', and fuel injection squirts the right amount of petrol in with the air as it goes into the cylinders. All this mechanism is packed away around the 911 engine in the standard engine compartment, itself a masterpiece of planning even apart from the technical expertise needed to produce an efficient turbocharging system. With high-pressure air and petrol going into the cylinders, more power is developed, and the higher the rpm of the engine the more boost pressure is available. Apart from the extra power, there are other advantages such as a much quieter exhaust note, a much smoother engine at all times, and a more efficient engine, which thereby results in improved fuel consumption. A pure racing engine is boosted to the highest pressure it can stand, for sheer power output, but a production road car has to make a compromise between power, fuel consumption and engine stress. The Porsche Turbo achieved an incredible balance of these factors.

The driver of a Porsche Turbo will immediately notice three things before he drives off. One is a small dial set into the rev-counter, which indicates boost pressure; the second is that the gearbox has only four speeds instead of the more normal five; and the third is the incredible smoothness and silence from behind, the turbine cutting out most of the exhaust noise. For the observant, there is another important point, and that is that the red line on the rev-counter is at 6,800 rather than at the more normal 7,200–400rpm. Although the turbocharger is running all the time that exhaust gases are emanating from the engine, it really starts to work at 3,500rpm, and from that point on things happen in a big way. The maximum power is delivered at 5,500rpm, so that 6,000rpm is more than enough, and with maximum torque at 4,000rpm the turbocharged Porsche engine proves to be a different beast altogether from the high-revving versions that went before.

If I had been impressed by the performance of the 2.7-litre Carrera RS, I was totally demoralized by the Porsche Turbo. It represented a whole new world of high-speed motoring, and moved into a realm that was really more than I could cope with under normal everyday conditions. Of course, you did not have to use all that power, nor let the engine develop its 12lb boost, but power corrupts . . . and I am easily corrupted. It would amble along at

A Passion for Porsches

120mph, while the enormous torque would waft it up to 135mph at a touch of the accelerator pedal. My first thought on seeing the 4-speed gearbox was that this was a retrograde step, but far from it: the power and torque were so enormous that gear-changing became superfluous. It would run to almost 120mph in third gear, while a change into fourth with 12lb boost would produce acceleration that was almost more than normal roads can manage to contain.

Everything happened so smoothly and quietly that it was deceptive. While taking a friend for a 'demo', I pulled out at about 80mph to overtake a row of cars and heard him suck his breath in apprehension. He had no idea of the performance of the car and was relating the speed and distance to his known parameters. I knew that the boost was rising and that it was all about to happen, and sure enough we went by that row of cars like a rocket, safely into the space ahead. It was his first taste of turbo-power and he was really impressed. On another trip, we were cruising along at just under the 100mph mark when we came up on an Alfa Romeo full of obvious motoring enthusiasts who recognized the Turbo, for it was the only one in the country at the time. Smiling and waving they watched us approach. They were doing 90mph or more, so I drew alongside them for a moment and then gave the Porsche full throttle. The way it gathered itself up and then effortlessly accelerated to 135mph impressed us, so it must have impressed those enthusiasts in the Alfa. I wasn't sure where I would have preferred to be: experiencing the high-speed acceleration of the Porsche Turbo, or in the Alfa, obviously flat out, seeing the white car disappear into the distance.

Porsche quoted the maximum speed of the Turbo as 155mph, but I never had the opportunity to find out. I certainly would not doubt their claims, even though such speed is fairly academic on the open road, apart from on an Autobahn. More important, however, is that such performance does mean that at reasonable speeds the car has a great deal in reserve, and 125mph cruising is effortless. Even when driven almost to the limit, it returns a remarkable 17mpg, and, as with all Porsches, the rest of the car is well up to the power of the engine. Porsche Engineering has always viewed the 911 as a whole, so that as more power is developed, better brakes are fitted, together with better wheels and tyres, improved suspension, greater stability all round, and so on.

The dictum of Porsche Engineering has always been to make their cars inherently safe, and not just crash-proof. Unlike most other manufacturers, they preach the gospel of 'primary safety'. By this they mean a car that is specifically designed not to have accidents, rather than one that is designed to lower standards and relies on being built like a battleship to make it safe when it does have an accident. Secondary safety naturally comes into the

In the mid-1970s, Belgian journalist Paul Frère was using a 911S as his regular transport around Europe. This model had now grown a tail spoiler. Later, when asked what was the best car in his experience, Frère answered without hesitation, 'the Porsche Turbo' (author).

Porsche design philosophy, but only after primary safety has been researched to the fullest.

While the 911 was reaching its peak in the Turbo version, another world was opening up at Zuffenhausen with the development of the 928 and 944, which would take the company well into the 1980s and 1990s. The 928 first appeared in the mid-1970s, overlapping with the 911 in much the same way as the 911 itself had overlapped with and then virtually eclipsed the 356 in 1963/4. But before we move into the world of the 928 and the 944, there is another development to relate in the saga of the 911. And that was the increase of engine capacity from 3.0 litres to 3.3 litres, still turbocharged.

It seemed almost unbelievable that all this capacity could still be contained within the same basic 911 body-shell. This had seemed much too big for a simple 2-litre engine when it first appeared, but now it seemed ridiculously small for the power of 3.3 litres of turbocharged engine, still in the original flat-6-cylinder configuration. While the 3.0-litre Turbo had seemed to be too much of everything, the 3.3-litre version was surely pure exaggeration, but then Porsche Engineering have always exaggerated: even the little 90mph

A Passion for Porsches

'beetle' 356 of 1950 was an exaggeration when compared to the 62mph Volkswagen from which it was born.

It was 1981 by the time I borrowed the 3.3-litre Turbo and four more years of traffic congestion and rules and regulations had been forced upon us. The only way to enjoy this ultimate 911 was to get up early before the world was astir and to revel in the total absurdity of the situation. It did not have any more ultimate power than the 3.0-litre Turbo, but it had an even wider spread of power and torque and its acceleration was such that it made you giggle with disbelief. I took Doug Nye, a very good friend of mine, for a run in it and when we stopped we both got out and leant on the car, giggling hysterically. We are both very experienced with fast, good cars, but we felt that the 3.3-litre Turbo Porsche was just another world which you could not explain to normal people. The modern world is not meant to be populated by such creatures. Reality is Mr Everyman in his Volkswagen Golf or his Ford

The 911 Porsche in its most extreme form in the shape of the 3.3-litre turbocharged version. For sheer exhilaration and the joy of motoring, this car takes a lot to beat. It made the author and his friend chuckle almost hysterically every time they used the full performance on acceleration.

The 911 grows up

Fiesta, not low-flying rockets like a Porsche Turbo. By 7.30am the world of Mr Everyman was beginning to stir, so I put the Porsche Turbo away and sat and watched what passes for motoring in the 1980s. There was little point in taking the Turbo out into the maelstrom of everyday traffic. It would have been like taking a Derby winner for a genteel trot in Hyde Park. Far better to keep it for special occasions when no one is looking, and to indulge in the purely selfish business of high-speed motoring, even if the time available is limited. There is nothing like self-indulgence, and the 3.3-litre Porsche Turbo was the greatest example yet to come from the Stuttgart factory. It was the ultimate 'Motoring Tool' and as such should be used only when you can motor with a capital M.

The 911 has come a long way since its inception, and I doubt if even the engineers at Porsche could have foreseen just how far it could be developed. Equally, I doubt if Ferry Porsche and his associates realized in 1948, when they were building the prototype 356, that it would develop as far as the 2-litre 356 Carrera that ended the original line. While the 911 is not yet ended, Porsche have moved into another world with the 928 and the 944, and in 10 or 15 years' time we shall probably look back on the 911 as an interesting step in Porsche Engineering development: a classic for its time, but outmoded by new developments.

Chapter
FIFTEEN

The 917

The creation of the Porsche model 917 was a very well kept secret until the factory were ready to release their bombshell on the sporting world. The management at the Zuffenhausen factory had undergone some drastic changes and Dr Ferry Porsche's nephew, Ferdinand Piëch, was in charge of research and development, guiding the engineering philosophy of the firm. He changed the whole technical aspect of Porsche. Until he took over, all Porsche competition – whether racing or rallying – was closely tied to production and the factory took part only in those categories for which they had an equivalent production model. They had started with the 1,100-cc class, gradually expanding into the 1,300-cc, 1,500-cc, 1,600-cc and 2,000-cc categories. While they were always successful within their class, they never bid for outright victory in the long-distance sports-car races. Ferdinand Piëch changed all that and his new engineering philosophy was to result in complete domination of the sports car world.

As this change was taking place, the rules governing sports car racing were relaxed to allow prototype one-off engines of 3 litres or limited production engines of 5 litres, the 'limit' of production being 25. Porsche had stretched their flat-6- and flat-8-cylinder engines as far as they could go. Even the 3-litre flat-8 was not a certain winner overall, and anyway had little development life left in it. In the most devastating exhibition of Porsche engineering prowess, the Zuffenhausen firm produced a totally new mid-engined sports/racing coupé with a 4½-litre 12-cylinder engine in two opposed rows of 6 cylinders. As with all Porsches up to this time, it was air-cooled and had a large cooling fan with plastic blades lying on top of the engine, blowing cooling air

The 917

The impressive line of 25 Porsche 917 coupés drawn up at the Zuffenhausen factory, awaiting inspection by CSI officials for homologation as 'production' sports cars for racing (Porsche Archives).

downwards across the cylinders and cylinder heads. To make one such engine experimentally would have been impressive, but when the Porsche management requested officials of the CSI, the governing body of motor sport, to visit the factory to inspect the model with a view to homologation as a production sports car, they had no less than 25 of these 12-cylinder coupés lined up outside the R & D department. Whether they were all complete and ready to run was academic, as was the question of whether they were all sold or intended to be sold. They were referred to either as the 'Nine-One-Seven' or the 'Nine-Seventeen'.

Previously, the largest and most powerful Porsche was the flat-8-cylinder 3-litre, used in the 908 series, so the introduction of a 500-hp 12-cylinder of 4½ litres, which was obviously intended for outright victory wherever it was to compete, set the sporting world buzzing with excitement. It had previously been thought that the 3-litre was stretching the limits of air-cooling beyond reasonable bounds, but now Porsche had produced an air-cooled 4½-litre.

A Passion for Porsches

The line-up of the 25 cars took place in April 1969, but I had heard about the new model in the autumn of 1968, in, of all places, a bar in Madrid. I was in Spain with the sporting element of the Reale Automovil Club d'Espagna and one night, or to be more accurate, very early one morning, I was having a drink with the Porsche importer for Spain, an expatriate German car dealer who also did a bit of rallying and racing with Porsche GT cars. In conversation he told me how he was negotiating to have one of the new 4½-litre Porsches for competition work in Spain. In view of the hour and the place, I did not take this story very seriously, especially as the only competition Porsches then available were of 3 litres only, and during the 1968 racing season I had not heard of any such Porsche. In fact, I forgot all about it until the official announcement was made and the first 917 coupé was shown at the Geneva Motor Show in March 1969. I then realized that my beery German friend had known what he was talking about.

Once the car had been accepted and homologated as a production sports/racing model, most of the 25 were dismantled and put in the stores as back-up material for the initial batch that was intended be raced. By the end of its racing life, more than 60 917s and variants had been built.

The ultimate version of the racing 917 coupé was the Gulf Oil sponsored car, in their blue and orange colours, with 5-litre twelve-cylinder engine (Porsche Archives).

The 917

The first were seen in action at the Le Mans 24 Hour race test weekend in March 1969. My lasting impression of that weekend was the look on the faces of the Porsche engineers, firstly when one car arrived back at the pits having sucked the perspex rear window out of its mounting on the long tapering tail and into the fan, and later when Hans Herrmann arrived back at the pits, after extending the car to its maximum down the Mulsanne Straight, with no trace of the horizontal cooling fan at all! The perspex window was really part of the engine cover, being positioned almost horizontally above the engine. After the first disaster, it had been removed altogether from Hans Hermann's car, and the fan had then become detached from its shaft and had taken off like a 'frisbee'.

The early test days of the 917 were very exciting, for the handling was not very good, certainly not good enough for the power of the engine, which had been quoted as 520bhp but was nearer 580bhp. It was an anxious time for the drivers on the fast but smooth Circuit de la Sarthe at Le Mans. When they got to the Nurburgring, in preparation for the ADAC 1,000 kilometre race, they were no longer very enthusiastic about driving this monster created by the Zuffenhausen engineers. The situation is best summed up by Ing Helmut Bott, who, on the night before the race, told his drivers, Frank Gardner and David Piper: 'To zee drivair who drives zee nine-one-seven in zee tousand kilometre rennen von Nurburgring – an Iron Cross. To zee drivair who finishes zee tousand kilometre rennen von Nurburgring – TWO Iron Cross.' The Porsche engineers had no illusions about their problems.

Eventually the 917 was tamed, to become one of the great sports/racing cars of all time, but not before John Woolf, one of the first customers, had been killed at Le Mans. This tragic accident was not really the fault of the 917, and the Porsche team had suggested to Woolf that his co-driver, the experienced Herbert Linge, should take the first driving stint. Unfortunately, John Woolf was desperately keen to drive the car in the race, even though his racing experience was very limited. In the opening laps, at a time when limits are fine and experience is all-important, he crashed fatally at the infamous White House bends.

It was John Wyer and his Gulf Oil Research team who guided Porsche on to the detailed aerodynamic route. With the back-up of Goodyear tyre technology, they overcame the 917's handling problems and from then on it became unassailable. Memories of Joseph Siffert, Pedro Rodriguez, Vic Elford and Helmut Marko in wheel-to-wheel battles with these fantastic cars come flooding back. I especially remember one episode at Monza when Siffert and Rodriguez were side by side past the grandstands as they caught up with and then lapped an Alfa Romeo Giulietta TZ, passing it one on each side. I never

A Passion for Porsches

At the Weissach Open Day there was much to see. This display of 911 racing components was typical, with a pair of 917 coupés in the background (Sloniger)

met the driver of that Alfa Romeo but he must have had a remarkable experience of relative speed.

As the 917 was developed, the capacity was increased to 5 litres and over 600hp was produced. After running normal long-distance 917 coupés in the Watkins Glen 6 Hour race in 1970, the John Wyer team ran one of the cars in the supporting Can-Am race over a brief 200 miles. The Canadian-American Challenge series in North America was the province of 7 or 8-litre Chevrolet powered sports/racing cars, tuned for a 200-mile event rather than a 6-hour, 12-hour or 24-hour event. However, the normal 917 coupé acquitted itself so well against such monsters that Porsche could see a new outlet for the car. One of the Can-Am supporters was Roger Penske, with his driver Mark Donohue, and they soon formulated a deal with Porsche to develop a Can-Am version of the 917 in open two-seater form. To boost the power above that of the big Chevrolet engines, Porsche increased the capacity to 5.4 litres and adopted exhaust-driven turbocharging. This development was in full swing at the Porsche research and development centre at Weissach

The 917

when the management agreed to hold an 'open day' for the sporting and technical Press.

The village of Weissach lies to the west of Stuttgart, out in the countryside, and it is just outside the village that Porsche have built their remarkable experimental establishment. I was at Monte Carlo for the Grand Prix, the weekend before this 'open day', when Huschke von Hanstein said, 'If you are passing Stuttgart on Tuesday, please call at Weissach to have a look round.' My plans were really geared to being in Stuttgart on Wednesday, but he insisted that it had to be Tuesday or not at all, and so I made other arrangements and arrived at Weissach on Tuesday morning, as requested. I had not realized that it was to be a very highly organized visiting day. It reminded me of when I worked at the Royal Aircraft Establishment at Farnborough during the war years. When the war in Europe was over, the Government agreed to allow the public in to RAE Farnborough to get an idea of what had been going on during the years 1939–45. All manner of exhibits were laid out, from German V2 rockets to supersonic testing equipment, and we all prepared for this invasion of engineering privacy and secrecy. It was exactly the same at Weissach. They showed us a good deal of interest, but it was obviously all out of date and obsolete work that was either routine or no longer secret. They did not show us what they were doing for the future, or what they were thinking about doing.

However, they did show us a turbocharged 917 engine on a test-bed, enclosed within a test-room and observed through a plate glass window. We were being conducted round in small groups and in my group was Jerry Sloniger, an American journalist friend who spoke fluent German and lived in Germany. The engineer in charge of the test-bed demonstration gathered us round the window and said, 'Ein moment, bitte'. We waited. Then, with a flourish, he pressed various switches and wound on a handle. Needles on dials and indicators moved and he said proudly, 'Ein towsand horsepower' – one thousand horsepower. We were all very impressed and never doubted his word: since a normal 917 engine could give 600hp, it seemed reasonable that a turbocharged one should give 1,000.

Engines have always fascinated me and I lingered with my American friend until the next group arrived. Once more, there was the flourish, the switches and knobs operated, and 'Ein towsand horsepower'. After a third demonstration I began to think that the turbo-charged 917 engine must be something very special to be capable of being run up to 7,000rpm and 1,000hp just like that, at the flick of a switch, especially as it all looked very placid when viewed through the glass window. After the engine had been shut down for the third time, a photographer wanted to take a close-up, and so the engineer in charge opened the door of the test-house to let him in. I could

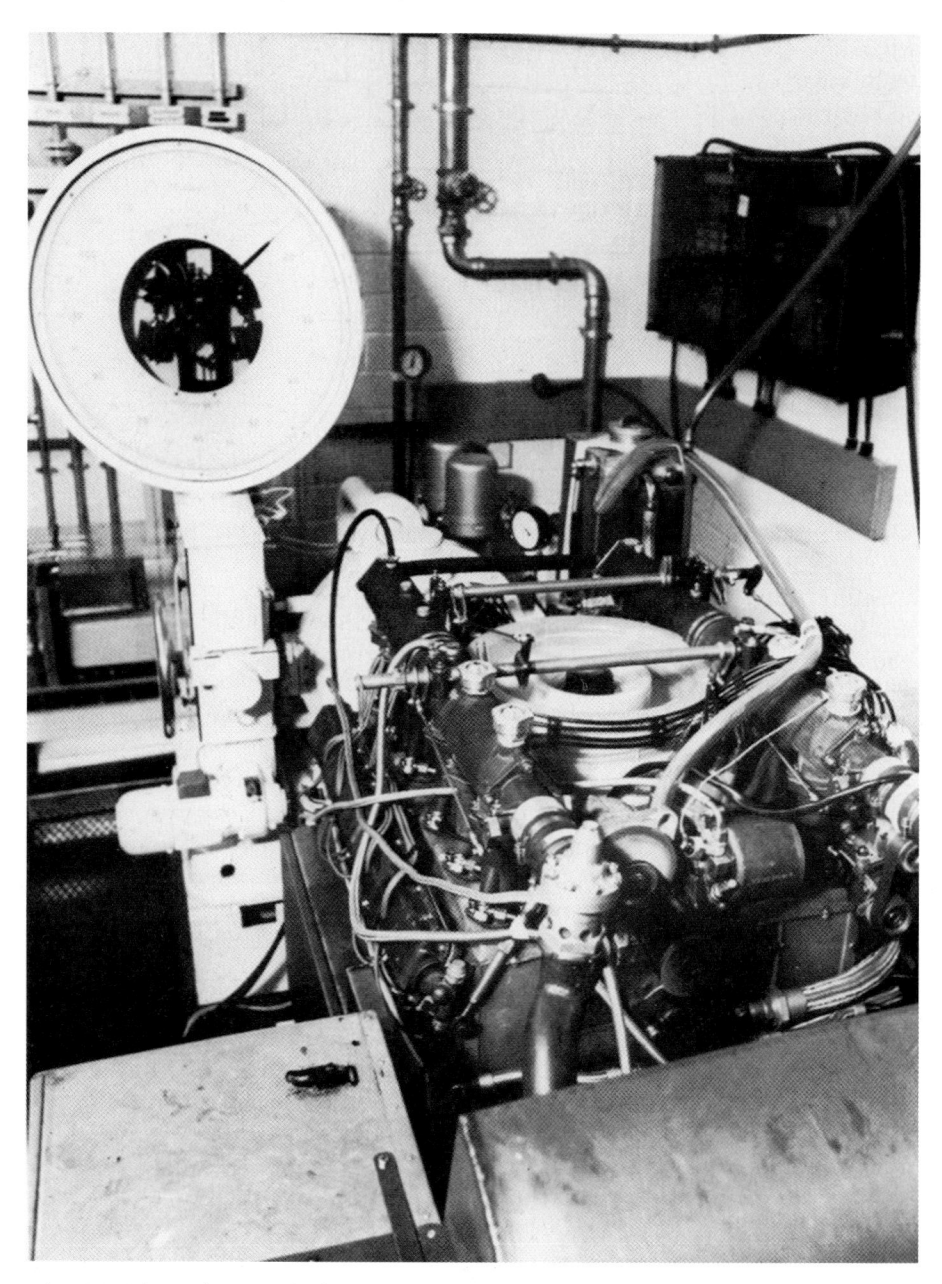

The 1,000-hp 917/10 turbocharged engine on one of the Weissach test beds (Porsche Archives).

not resist joining him, just to experience the pleasure of standing by an engine that had just produced 1,000hp. The air in the test chamber was very cool and there was no heat coming from the now stationary 917 engine – after three runs in quick succession to 'Ein towsand horsepower'. I am not saying that the engine was driven by an electric motor, for exhibition purposes, but I do recall some of the subterfuges we got up to at RAE Farnborough when we let the public in to ogle at what was going on.

As I have said, I have always been fascinated by powerful engines, and I used to enjoy going into the RAE engine test-beds when a Napier Sabre was pushing out 4,000hp or a Bristol Centaurus 3,000. I find such machinery awe-inspiring. With the aid of my American friend and my limited German, we discussed the turbocharged 917 Porsche engine, for I was interested to know what the Porsche engineers had had to do when they raised the output from 500/600 to 1,000hp. On the face of it, it had been a simple matter to fit a turbocharger unit into the exhaust system, supply the engine with compressed air from the turbo-compressor, inject the petrol, and 'hey presto' – 1,000hp. At least, that was the impression given to the visitors to the Weissach research and development centre. However, there is no way it could be as easy as that, for a racing engine is a simple heat-engine and heat is relative to power, and heat has to be dissipated. It was admitted that a larger oil cooler was used, and that the rate of flow of oil through the larger oil cooler was greatly increased, so that although the 917 Turbo was still air-cooled on the face of it, it was in fact oil-cooled, as most Porsche racing engines had been for some time.

The other thing that intrigued me about the 917 Turbo engine was the question of internals and moving parts. The original 917 engine had been designed as a racing unit so it was reasonable to assume that the crankshaft, pistons, connecting rods, valves, valve gear and so on had been designed and stressed with a suitable safety factor for 500hp. If the same engine now produced 1,000hp in turbocharged form, then either the internals were running dangerously low on safety, or the original design was absurdly robust for a racing unit. After some discussions with the engineer in charge of the 917 Turbo demonstration unit, I did get him to admit that 'many pieces' had had to be changed, or redesigned, and it was clear that the 917/10 engine did not happen overnight. The point of all this interest on my part was to determine just how serious this Can-Am project was. It was serious, all right. Development had been going on for a long while before we were shown the turbocharged engine: it was not just a simple matter of fitting a turbocharger and producing nearly twice as much power.

After our trip round the facilities of Weissach, we were taken out on to the test-track, past an intriguing pair of production Porsches carrying out 'urban

A Passion for Porsches

The remarkable mechanism installed in a 911 on the 'rolling road' to operate the controls during endurance testing for the urban cycle (Sloniger).

cycle' tests. In California a set of standards have been drawn up for a typical commuter journey to work. This involves starting, stopping, cruising slowly, short bursts of acceleration, stopping, starting, and so on, simulating the morning grind to work in heavy traffic. Under United States laws, a car has to reach a certain standard of exhaust emission and fuel consumption for this 'urban cycle'. These two Porsches were set up on rolling-road dynamometers with electro-magnetic gear coupled to the controls, operating the accelerator, clutch and brake pedals, as well as the gearbox. It was fascinating to watch these cars repeating all the motions of a morning drive into Los Angeles, out in the open, with no one inside or even standing nearby. They were left running for hours on end. Occasionally a mechanic would arrive with a jerrycan of petrol and top up the fuel tanks while the cars motored unconcernedly along on their programmed course. To design the mechanical linkage for operating the controls would have been complicated enough, to say nothing of the electronic gear to operate it all.

The purpose of our visit out on to the very elaborate test track was to see the huge skid-pan where handling and cornering characteristics are

The 917

The Weissach research and development test-track seen from the air, with the technical buildings in the bottom right-hand corner (Porsche Archives).

studied. Here we were confronted by a 917/10 with open two-seater bodywork – the prototype Can-Am car, with turbocharged horizontally opposed 12-cylinder engine and 'ein towsand horsepower'. Mark Donohue was testing the car on the circular steering test-track and it became very clear that Porsche were tackling Can-Am racing with the same seriousness that they applied to everything else. The only sad thing about it all was that the addition of the turbocharger to the exhaust system made the engine incredibly quiet, which seemed all wrong for a 1,000-hp racing car. The normal 917 had a very healthy bark to its exhaust, but the 917/10 was dull by comparison.

On our return to the assembly area of the test-track, a racing 917 coupé was produced and those of us who were interested were offered a ride round the track in the passenger seat. This was an experience not to be missed. The driver was the works test-driver and master-mechanic, Hubert Mimmler. Some journalists who were not close to Porsche and racing did not know Hubert, but I had known him from the early days of the 550 Spyder, the Targa Florio, the Nurburgring, and numerous European circuits. He was

Hubert Mimmler, master mechanic and test-driver at the Weissach research centre (Porsche Archives).

The 917

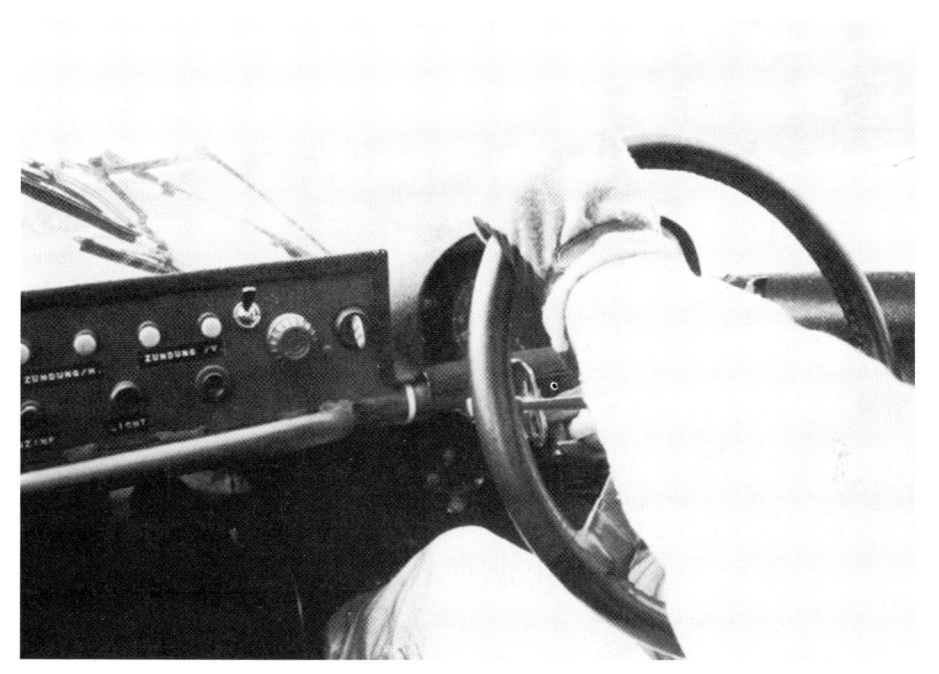

The view from the passenger seat in the 917 during a test-run with Hubert Mimmler on the Weissach track (Sloniger).

now spending much of his time test-driving round Weissach and probably knew it – and the 917 – better than anyone. Thus, we had no need of a 'racing ace' to give us a good impression of the car.

Space in the tiny cockpit was very limited and you had your feet sticking out ahead of the front wheels. In fact, you were very conscious of the proximity of the left front wheel to your left knee, with only a sheet of aluminium and some tubes protecting you as you lay back in the seat. To say that a ride in a 917 coupé was exciting and impressive is to put it very mildly. It was shattering. For the first time in many years of high speed motoring, I became very conscious of the part that a single tyre was playing in my destiny. As we took the right-hand corners at something around 120–130 mph, I was terribly aware that all that existed between us and kingdom-come was the adhesion and grip being offered by the left front tyre close to my knee. I could not help thinking philosophically, 'I hope that tyre does not burst.' I find you have to take that sort of view when being driven right on the limit of safety, as otherwise you simply become frightened. As I love racing cars, I have no intention of being frightened by them, so I am quite happy analysing

The 917/10 turbocharged Can-Am prototype on test on the Weissach research track (Porsche Archives).

things as they happen. It was the same when Hubert was braking heavily from 140mph. I could see his strong right leg really pressing on the brake pedal and feel the tyres gripping the road as the deceleration forces tried to throw us forward. If the brakes had suddenly failed, we would have finished up a long way across country from Weissach.

That ride was an experience I shall always remember and it rounded off a superbly interesting day. Before we left we had the opportunity of a long discussion with Professor Fuhrmann, who was then head of Porsche Engineering. When the management bade us good-bye, they said, 'We have been pleased to show you our research facilities, but now we have much work to do so we would ask you not to come back.' In fact, I had enjoyed the day so much and was so full of excitement, that when I drove off, I left my overcoat behind in the canteen cloakroom! I never went back, so it is probably still there.

The 917/10 and subsequent 917/30 Porsche models virtually destroyed Can-Am racing through 'over kill'. It had been a fairly simple, amateurish activity until Porsche arrived on the scene. They dominated it so conclusively

The 917

that the Americans rewrote the rules to outlaw the 1,000-hp Porsche Can-Am cars. This was a pity, for Porsche were working on a serious engine for Can-Am racing, a new 16-cylinder with two rows of 8 cylinders horizontally opposed. This monster power unit even had the Porsche engineers twitching a bit during test-bed sessions. They remarked in all seriousness, because Porsche engineers are serious people, 'Vee haf made our calculations, und mit turbo-lader vee could haf 2,000 horsepower from our 16-cylinder engine.' It's a pity the Americans outlawed it all, for that sort of power would have made the bravest driver's eyes water a bit. The project was abandoned and today one of the engineers has a 16-cylinder crankshaft standing on end in his office and uses it as a hat-stand.

When the 917 long-distance racing project ended, this time when the FIA changed the rules because Porsche had become too dominant, one of the cars was prepared for road use, with interior trim, regulation lights and silencing, and so on. This was carried out at the request of Count Gregorio Rossi, one of the brothers who own the Martini-Rossi drinks consortium, who had put a lot of money into sponsoring the works 917 team during its hey-day. As the ultimate road-car, this 917 took some beating. Naturally enough, it did not get a lot of use – but what a lovely thing to own!

Chapter SIXTEEN

Another World

The first indication that Porsche knew something about cars with engines cooled by water and not mounted at the rear came in 1976, though very much as an aside to what seemed to be happening. To anyone thinking ahead, it was clear that though the Porsche Turbo was a magnificent beast, it really had to be the end of the 911 line, and the problem was, 'where to go from there?'. Racing Porsches had shown that the firm could make superlative flat-8-cylinder and flat-12-cylinder engines, but their very size meant that they had to be mounted amidships, between the cockpit and the rear axle. Although many firms had tried, no-one had come up with the complete answer to a mid-engined layout for a road car. No-one would question a mid-engined, two-seater layout for a competition car, or a small production run 'fun-car', but Porsche production was geared to much larger markets, and the success of these markets ensured continuation of their racing activities and vice-versa. If they had been interested in producing a mid-engined sports car in small quantities, they would have put the 904 into production, and in any case they had burnt their fingers slightly with the abortive VW-Porsche 914. Their racing flat-8 engine in the 907 was an impressive piece of engineering, and the flat-12 917 was an all-time classic and an engineering 'tour de force', but at no time did they show any sign of marketing a line-production model based on either engine.

I did once meet a man who claimed to have seen a prototype, flat-8-cylinder, mid-engined, road-going Porsche coupé in, of all places, Greece! The interesting thing was that he was not a sporting motorist and knew nothing of Porsche cars or their racing activities, but did know someone in the

Another World

Porsche company's financial management. In all innocence, and only because I happened to be in a Porsche at the time, he mentioned his business associate being in Greece in a Porsche, '. . . a very special car, I believe, with a racing 8-cylinder engine . . .' I got no further as he did not even know that Porsches were air-cooled and rear-engined. I never did get to the bottom of that little snippet of information.

So, where to go from the ultimate 911, apart from making another 'ultimate' 911? By no logic or reasoning could one arrive at an answer, and certainly no Porsche enthusiast envisaged the direction in which Porsche thinking was going.

The Weissach research and development centre was busy on a project for Audi-NSU, to create a sports coupé using existing Audi components

The 924 Porsche presented an entirely new image for the Stuttgart firm, which was to herald the Porsches for the 1980s and 1990s in the shape of the 944 and the 928S. While using many Audi components, the 924 was built to Porsche standards. The main headlamps are concealed under flaps on the nose.

A Passion for Porsches

In line with their normal policy of development, it was not long before a Carrera version of the 924 was made available. The flared wheel arches over the wider tyres was a foretaste of the 944 which was to follow.

wherever possible. This project was no surprise, for Ferdinand Piëch had moved from Porsche to Audi-NSU and it will be remembered that he was Dr Porsche's nephew. He had taken his inventiveness and engineering knowledge to the moribund Audi firm and was revitalizing it in a most impressive manner. When Porsche had completed the design of the sports Audi, using an improved Audi 4-cylinder water-cooled engine at the front and a Porsche-designed trans-axle at the rear, and incorporating as many production components as possible, the management of Audi-NSU underwent a complete change and the new directors decided to drop the idea of an Audi sports car. As far as Porsche were concerned, it had really gone too far to be scrapped, so they made a deal with Audi to put the car into production at the Neckarsulm NSU plant. And so the Porsche 924 was born. It wasn't as simple as that in reality, for much of the design of the 924 had stemmed from research on a far more ambitious Porsche project.

Another World

This was the 928. It was audacious in both design and conception, considering that the world was still reeling from the decision of the 'oily boys' in the Middle East to take command of their very desirable ground product, to the detriment of everyone's inflation. Even those who had an inkling of what Porsche were designing found it hard to believe. Air-cooling was abandoned, as was rear engine mounting, two basic concepts of Porsche design since 1948. It seemed incredible that Porsche Engineering were going to start on a whole new line of development, but start they did, and with a conviction that was not only staggering but the envy of many other manufacturers. While the 928 design was being finalized and programmed for production, the 924 project was put on the market in 1976. Whether it was fortuitous or the result of good planning, the Audi-based, water-cooled, front-engined, rear-wheel-drive car prepared the world of Porsche owners for the shattering blow that was to be delivered a year later.

The 911 was still in full cry, with all versions selling well, but the Porsche management knew that the motoring scene was changing rapidly due to social and economic influences. A more sophisticated type of sporting car was

An early 928 Porsche that the author had out on test. The headlamps are in the 'on' position; when switched off, they lay back pointing mutely to the sky. The alloy road wheels of bizarre design were typical of the 'new world' Porsche (author).

going to be required to meet the future demands of the world's markets. Although the 928 was released early in 1977, Porsche made it clear that it was a car for the 1980s, just as the 911 had been a car for the 1970s when it was introduced in the mid-1960s. No true Porsche owner was interested in the 924, and Porsche did not really expect them to be, for the various 911 models catered for their needs admirably, but it was hoped that the fairly conventional 924 would attract new people into the Porsche market and prepare them for the new model to come. The 928 was something altogether different, opening up a new world of fast, safe motoring. Although the specification on paper seemed fairly orthodox, the engineering was far from it, breaking new ground at every turn of the design.

To keep in touch with this 'new world', I first of all tried a bog-standard 924. It did nothing for me at all. True, it seemed to be quite nicely made, but the 4-cylinder engine was gutless and fussy if revved hard, rather like an average Ford engine. In true Porsche style, the 924 was improved rapidly. One big step forward was the replacement of the 4-speed gearbox by a 5-speed unit, which instantly made the car more usable as a sports coupé. Later on, a turbocharged version and then a Carrera version were added to the range, each a good step forward, but neither very startling because the base line had been so low to begin with. In the interim, the 928 had arrived, and the 924 series paled into insignificance.

Whereas the styling of the 924 was a bit unusual and not at all characteristic of Porsche, the 928 was different again, but so functionally aggressive that you just had to stand in awe of it. While it was bulbous and Germanic, it was totally devoid of 'gimickery' and flashiness, almost to the point of being extreme. It was certainly functional, and when it was placed alongside the 911 Turbo with its spoilers, flared wheel arches, aerodynamic wings and so on, its subdued shape was undoubtedly impressive. Packed away under the bonnet was a 4.5-litre water-cooled V8 engine that bristled with interesting design features. The 5-speed gearbox was in unit with the rear axle assembly and ahead of it, giving good weight distribution. At first glance it seemed to be a big car, but there was no wasted space anywhere and it was after all a 4.5-litre V8. Once behind the wheel and out in the road, you were no longer conscious of its size, for it had superb steering, an incredibly small turning circle and very little overhang anywhere, the wheels being very much at the corners.

While the Porsche Turbo was a riot of fun and a wonderful machine for 'letting off steam', even if it was a bit anti-social, the 928 had nearly the same performance with none of the inherent excitement. It was not dull, far from it, but it did not excite like the hot 911 cars did. There was none of the joy of pulling 7,500rpm in third, as on the 911S, and then snatching the gear lever into fourth with the engine singing away. The 928 could do all that in top

The 928S with air-dam under the nose and small spoiler below the rear window. The new style of alloy road wheel is a lot less fussy than the original design (Porsche Archives).

gear, with so much torque that the rev-counter was almost superfluous. It wasn't an old-fashioned Porsche and it wasn't supposed to be. It represented a whole new concept of high speed motoring: you felt that the engineers at Weissach who designed it must have kept trying the ultimate 911, and saying to themselves, 'there is a better and more efficient way of doing things'. After all, we were approaching the 1980s and Porsche were already looking ahead to the world of motoring in the 1990s.

When I drove that first 928 I was unsure whether I liked it or not, but such was my admiration for Porsche Engineering that I had to say to myself, 'Hold on, this is the beginning of a new era, not the end. Obviously they will develop the 928 like they developed the 911 and the 356 before it, so let us wait and see.' The ride, road-holding, steering and braking were all of a very high order, and so efficient and functional that you kept saying to yourself, 'It can't really be this good': but it was. The Porsche power steering, so necessary with the modern wide-tread tyres, surpassed even the standards previously set by Citroën and Daimler-Benz. The 928's looks began to grow on me very quickly, not so much for their elegance or excitement, like a Dino Ferrari, but for their sheer functional arrogance. The car seemed to be saying, 'I'm not this shape because it is pretty or tantalizing; I'm this shape because I am functional and efficient, and I am ready for the 1980s.' There was something almost smug about the character exuded by the 928. You felt that if you didn't respect it you would be castigated by a superior power.

It did not take Weissach long to come up with an S version. The engine capacity was increased from just under 4.5 litres to just over, and internal modifications produced 300 DIN hp, which is real horsepower and not sales and publicity horsepower. More staggering was the increase in the torque figure, from 257lb/ft at 3,600rpm to 283lb/ft at 4,500rpm. The peak power was at 5,900rpm, but with all that torque available there was no need to go much over 5,500. 300 usable horsepower in the 928S was a far cry from the 70hp of the original 356S, and everything else had progressed to the same degree.

By the time I had the chance to borrow a 928S, I was already well indoctrinated into the 'new world' and was very appreciative of it, for technical reasons more than anything else. The shape had grown on me so much that when I went to the Reading headquarters of Porsche Cars Ltd and saw a row of 928s parked outside, with a 911 Turbo amongst them, my instant reaction was, 'what's that funny looking thing?' This might seem sacrilegeous

A number plate that speaks for itself on the 'demonstrator' 928S belonging to Porsche Cars Great Britain Ltd, which the author used for a trip to the West Country (author).

Another World

to a pure Porsche enthusiast, until one remembers that seeing a 356 in a row of 911s in 1964 inspired exactly the same sort of reaction.

I was lucky enough to be able to borrow the 928S soon after I had tried the 3.3-litre Turbo 911, and so was able to make some pretty direct comparisons. There is nothing quite like the sheer urge of the Turbo 911 as the compressor pressure rises, but the 928S provides the same result with no drama whatsoever, while its ride and cornering ability are superior. Indeed, I don't think it is possible for a normal person to reach the limit of its roadholding under ordinary road conditions, and anyone who has an accident in a 928S must be an unmitigated idiot. With all that horsepower and torque, the 5-speed gearbox seemed superfluous, and with its very high cornering power I often found I was far too busy to contemplate a gear change, especially on winding roads. The next stop has got to be the elimination of the gearbox and the substitution of an infinitely variable step-less transmission. Already the 5-speed gearbox is being phased out in preference to the Porsche/Daimler-Benz 3-speed automatic transmission. The 928S was the first car on which I would have been prepared to accept an automatic transmission in place of a gearbox.

I have stressed the fact that the shape of the 928S is functional and not stylized, and this was brought home to me when I had the chance to take it up to 135–140mph. Under the same conditions, I was able to achieve this same speed in the 3.3-litre Turbo 911, neither car being at its absolute maximum, but fast enough for my peace of mind. In the Turbo 911 you had to concentrate and were constantly making small steering corrections to keep the car in a straight line. It never wandered about, but it felt as if it was on 'tippy-toes' and slightly 'nervous'. At the same speed on the same road, the 928S just sat there fatly. There seemed to be no need to hold the steering wheel, and certainly no need to make any steering corrections. The 911 Turbo achieves its speed through a triumph of engineering over technical adversity, while the 928S achieves it through the fundamental perfection of the design and shape. It imparts this feeling to the driver in a big way: you can almost hear it saying, 'I told you I was functional.'

If I had to choose between the two cars for a three-hour 'thrash', I would take the 911 Turbo every time, for the sheer adrenalin-flowing fun of it, but if I had to drive from London to Munich in a hurry I would take the 928S. I am sure that that is exactly what the Porsche engineers had in mind when they set out to provide another new generation of Porsche motoring. Whenever I see a 928S amongst ordinary cars, I cannot stop myself thinking, 'Look at that fat sod; it knows it is the best.' What the 928 will be like when it has had as much development as the 911, or the 356 before that, hardly bears thinking about.

An original right-hand-drive production 944 Porsche, photographed before it had even been spoilt by the addition of a proper number plate. The headlamps rise from under the flaps on the nose, the spot lamps within the front bumper being used for 'flashing' (Porsche Archives).

As I was completing the writing of this book, Porsche introduced another new car, the 944, based on knowledge gained with the 928 and the 924. An experimental 944 had been raced at Le Mans in 1981 and had finished seventh overall, spending less time on pit stops than any other competitor. It was fast, rugged and reliable. In the autumn the new car was announced and right-hand-drive versions were due in Great Britain early in 1982. The first right-hand-drive model duly arrived when Porsche Cars Great Britain Ltd's man, Mike Cotton, drove it back from Stuttgart. Through one of those lucky chances, as so often happened with me where Porsches were concerned, I happened to be in the right place at the right time, and met Mike the day he arrived back with the new car. He was bubbling over with enthusiasm, even though his trip had been through awful weather and the 944 was covered in mud and grime. In looks it was a cross between the 924 and the 928, smooth without being elegant, but not so aggressive and functional as the 928. However, what had impressed Mike was the smoothness of the 2.5-litre 4-cylinder engine and its torque and power characteristics.

A Porsche 944 at speed on a motorway – a shape that is fast becoming very familiar. Once the car was in full production, a rubbing strip was added to the door panel to protect it from other people in car parks (Porsche Archives).

Porsche plans for introducing the car in Great Britain involved quite an interesting exercise. This first 'demonstrator' was taken round to all the most important dealers, and a little while later the first batch of production cars arrived at Reading. These were passed on to the dealers who took them on as 'demonstrators'. Each dealer then ran the car in thoroughly, at the same time evaluating customer reaction. In the spring, Porsche Cars arranged a Press day for motoring writers to meet the 944. A number of the dealers' 'demonstrators' was assembled at Reading, all nicely bedded in and ready for serious use, and the motoring writers each took a car on a suggested route to the West Country for lunch and then returned to Reading, covering around 200 miles. There were no restrictions on how they drove, the exact route they took, or the types of roads they used, so a good cross-section of motoring ensued, from country lanes to motorway. A fuel check was made at the end of the day, as one of many attributes of this new Porsche product was its good fuel consumption.

Although I knew about this day out a long time before, I could not fit it in

A Passion for Porsches

to my plans and arranged to have a run in a 944 at a later date. In fact, I had forgotten all about it by the time it was due. Quite by chance, I called in at the Reading Porsche headquarters to see John Aldington, the son of H. J., who is now the head of the firm, to discuss something totally remote from Porsches. As I arrived, I noticed two or three shiny 944 coupés and a couple of journalistic people that I knew. Having forgotten about the test day, I

The very advanced and highly efficient Porsche 944 engine which is canted over to the right when installed, this view being from the front. A toothed belt within the front cover drives the balance shafts one on each side of the block (Porsche Archives).

Another World

wondered what was happening. When I asked to see Mr Aldington, I was told he was in the West Country, at which point Mike Cotton appeared and said, 'Why don't you drive down in a 944 and see him?' I had planned a very busy day on other things, but as so often happens, motoring was the priority and work came second. As one of the journalists had failed to arrive, there was a spare 944 available, so I took the keys gratefully and set off to catch up with the others before lunch.

The car was the 'demonstrator' of Malaya Garages of Billingshurst in Sussex. It was pale blue with a 5-speed manual gearbox, there being an automatic transmission option available. When driving the various versions of the 924, you were always conscious of the fact that the car was not a true Porsche, and you tended to keep saying to yourself, 'This is very good for a sports Audi, and some things are pure Porsche, but the overall package is not terribly impressive.' The 944 was a different thing altogether. The basic layout was from the 'new world' of Porsche, with a water-cooled 4-cylinder engine at the front, a propeller shaft enclosed within a torque tube, and the 5-speed gearbox in unit with the final drive. It was equipped with all round independent suspension, disc brakes, fuel injection and all the modern technicalities that Porsche had designed into the 928. As it is only half the size of the 928, and is powered, in fact, by almost half a 928 engine, the performance was not shattering, but what there was came smoothly and efficiently, following the 'new world' concept. The 4-cylinder engine is endowed with two contra-rotating balance shafts running at twice the engine speed to cancel out the inherent vibrations of a 4-cylinder engine, and this they do very effectively. If there wasn't the traditional, large, clear rev-counter, you would be hard put to guess what sort of rpm the engine was doing at any speed. It cruised effortlessly at 110–120mph, with such remarkable torque characteristics that even in fifth gear it surged forward at 100mph in an impressive manner – not in the manner of a 911 Turbo or 928S, naturally enough, but impressive for the 2.5-litre car that it is. The gearbox, controlled by a short stubby lever, is a delight, and the whole manner of going so obviously stems from the 928S that it really is a 'little brother'.

Already the 924 is being phased out of the American market and the 944 has taken over. If we view the 924 as a 'softener' to introduce the 'new world' of Porsche, we can see that it served its purpose admirably. The 928 and the 928S set the seal of Porsche in the 1980s and 1990s, and the 944 now formed a first-class stepping stone for anyone warily setting out on the Porsche path.

The days of the riotous 911 are obviously numbered, although while there are people to buy them in sufficient numbers they will still be made, and the 911 Turbo must stand for all time as a Porsche pinnacle. In years to come,

The driving seat of the Porsche 944. True to Porsche tradition, it is designed for driving, not just for sitting in (Porsche Archives).

when the ultimate Porsche is a 5.5-litre twin-turbocharged version of the 928, with infinitely variable transmission, anti-lock braking, hydro-pneumatic self-levelling suspension and many other improvements that are probably already in the Weissach pipeline, it will be interesting to look back on the fun days of the 911 Turbo and see how Porsche have progressed. When the 2-litre Carrera 356 was introduced, it seemed to be the 'ultimate' Porsche, and it was quite impossible to visualize the 911 Turbo in any shape or form. The 928 of 10 or 15 years' hence is just as hazy.

Chapter SEVENTEEN

Porsche Today

As we have seen in the previous chapter, the production Porsches are well on their way into the 1980s with two solid lines of development, the V8-cylinder 928 and its variants, and the 4-cylinder 944. However, Porsche Engineering does not stand still, and research and development continues apace on all manner of projects. At the Weissach research and development centre, more than 1,000 people are now employed, carrying out research for the German government and for some of the world's most important car manufacturers. Obviously, no details are ever released about work being done for other car manufacturers, but it is no secret that the facilities at Weissach are almost limitless. With the known engineering ability of the firm of Porsche and their natural integrity, it is not surprising that many firms make use of these facilities, in the sure knowledge that total secrecy and discretion will prevail.

Apart from carrying out research work for their own production line, the people at Weissach are also very involved in racing, for the Porsche firm has always believed that 'racing improves the breed' and is the fastest form of practical development. Until 1982, all racing development was done in a corner of the main facility, with people from various departments joining in as required. Now a separate racing department has been built in the centre of the test track, divorced from the everyday work of Weissach, but obviously closely in touch. For the 1982 season, Porsche returned to racing in the long-distance endurance category with a full-blooded factory team. After a singleton entry won the Group C category at the Silverstone Six Hours Race, the full force of the factory was directed to the Le Mans 24 Hour Race. They

A Passion for Porsches

The research and development centre of Porsche Systems Engineering at Weissach, where 1,000 people are employed; the facilities are the envy of motor manufacturers world-wide (Porsche Archives).

made a clean sweep of the event with the latest Porsche 956, a twin-turbo 2.65-litre flat-6-cylinder with oil and water cooling and very little air cooling, developing 600hp. The team was backed financially by Rothmans, and once more demonstrated the prowess of Porsche Engineering to the world at large. The three cars entered finished in first, second, and third places, something that is difficult to improve upon! Even though the opposition was not very strong, reliability is all important, and reliability has been one of the tenets of Porsche thinking since the days of Professor Ferdinand and his Volkswagen.

As these words are being printed, an interesting new venture is taking shape in the design offices of Weissach, in the form of a turbocharged 1½-litre Formula One engine for Grand Prix racing. This will not be fitted in a Porsche car, but in a McLaren, sponsored by Marlboro and Techniques d'Avant Garde (TAG), a Saudi Arabian firm who are into all branches of industrial technology. Although details of the engine have not yet been released, other than it being an 80-degree V6 using new materials technology, designed to give something like 650hp and at the same time to provide better

The official Porsche factory team returned to Le Mans in 1982 with the 956 model, sponsored by Rothmans cigarettes, with the usual technical help from Dunlop, Shell petrol, Bosch, Bilstein shock-absorbers and KKK turbochargers. They achieved a sweeping 1-2-3 with this car finishing first, driven by Jacky Ickx and Derek Bell.

The successful Marlboro-sponsored McLaren MP4B of 1982 powered by the Cosworth DFV engine. With a Porsche turbocharged power unit, its successor should be a worthy contender for World Championship honours (Marlboro).

A Passion for Porsches

The author chatting to Dr Ferry Porsche about 'Porsche in the 1980s' on the occasion of the opening of the new headquarters of Porsche Cars Great Britain Ltd at Reading in 1977 (Porsche Archives).

fuel consumption than those turbocharged engines built by BMW, Ferrari and Renault and used during 1982.

It is interesting to recall a conversation I had with Porsche engineers, including Ing Helmut Bott who is now head of research, about 10 years ago. I asked if Porsche would ever consider returning to Formula One Grand Prix racing, recalling their brief foray in the early 1960s. Their collective response was, 'only if we have to', and as they said that they smiled and looked towards the east and Munich, the home of BMW. It could just be coincidence that 1982 saw a full-time entry into Grand Prix racing by BMW, with their 4-cylinder turbocharged engine in a Brabham chassis, while at the same time McLaren International announced that they had concluded a deal with Porsche for the supply of a Grand Prix engine for 1983. McLaren International is now run by Ron Dennis, while responsibility for design is in

The range of Porsche cars driven and experienced by the author are illustrated by the 356A of 1955 and 944 of 1982 (356A: author; 944: Porsche Archives).

the capable hands of John Barnard. The origins of the firm go back to nearly 20 years ago, when it was started by Bruce McLaren. After his unfortunate death in a testing accident, his co-directors kept the firm going and eventually it amalgamated with the racing team of Ron Dennis. The 1982 McLaren Formula One car has been very successful and must be a good basis for the new Porsche–McLaren project.

The whole concept of Porsche cars and Porsche Engineering has come a very long way since 1948, when Ferry Porsche, Karl Rabe and Irwin Komenda planned the first post-war sports car, while Professor Ferdinand was being held in jail by the French military authorities. Although old Professor Porsche sowed the seeds of what was to become a remarkable empire, it was his brilliant son Ferry who really got things going and who guided the firm along the lines established by his father. Over the years, others have taken command of Porsche Engineering, but its standards and effectiveness would have met the approval of the old Professor at each stage of its development. Over a span of 34 years, the Porsche empire has grown to unimaginable heights, but throughout those years the cornerstone has been 'integrity'. Basic straight-forward engineering has been the guiding light and the firm has always built sports cars as modern as the day – cars which are always a pleasure to drive and which are designed for just that purpose. The very first Porsche was designed for the driver to drive, and the same holds good for the production cars of today. While Porsche thinking has always been geared to racing, the results and benefits of such development have always been fed back into the production line. One favourite Porsche saying is, 'Driving in its purest form'. That sums up Porsche cars, as I have experienced them. Nothing has changed at Zuffenhausen, apart from the fact that Porsche cars are now 34 years better than the original split windscreen 356 coupés

I have been very fortunate to have had such a long and happy association with the Porsche firm. I can look back with pleasure on experiences with something like 35 different models. Regrettably, I cannot look forward to the next 35 models from Dr hc F. Porsche KG, but I hope to keep in touch with as many as I can before my motoring days are finished.

Index

page numbers in *italics* refer to illustrations

Abridge Aerodrome (Ess.), 74
acceleration, 153 160–1, 166
accessories, 36
accidents, 44, 51, *119*, 132–6, 140–1, 144, 167, 173
AFN Ltd, 28, 29, 32, 33, 35, 155
airborne at speed, 71–2
airflow, 136, 137, *139*, 140, 162
Aldington, H. J. (Aldy), 28, 35, 194
Aldington, John, 194
Aldington, W. H. (Bill), 28, 155
Alexander, Jesse, 45–9, 53, 54–7, 82–3, 136, *137*, 140–1
Alfa Romeo cars, 13, 15, 173–4
Arctic motoring, 111, *112*
Ashdown, Peter, 68
Audi-NSU, 13, 185–6
Austria, driving in, 94, *96*–7
Auto Union *P-wagen*, 13–21
V16, 15, 17, 18
V12, 19
Axis race 1939, 22, 23

badges, *40*, 41
Barnard, John, 202
Barth, Edgar, 80, 87
Behra, Jean, 53, 113–16

Bekaert, John, 68
Bell, Derek, *199*
Berlin–Rome race 1939, 22, 23
Biesenberger, Hortolf, 142–4
birds, hitting, 136–8
Birkett, Holland, 63
Bloxham, Jean, 68
bodies, *118*, 123, *143*
Bohm, Hermann, *26*, 27
Bohringer, Eugen, 126–7
Bonnier, Joakim, 79, 80
Bott, Helmut, 173, 200
brakes, 130, 163
Brands Hatch, 74
Buchet, Robert, 53
Bugatti cars, 13, 63–4
bumpers, 51
Burke, Jack, 49–51, 53, 64–5, *69*, 71, 74, 77, 78, 141
Burke, Pat, *50*, *78*
Burn, Michael, 29, 32, 33, 34, 61–4, 67
Burnett, Sandy, 32, 140

Cabriolet model, 37, *39*, 142
Californian Road Runners, 53
cams, 58
Can-Am race, 174, 177, 179, 182–3

203

Carnegie, Robin, 68
Carrera model, 49–51, 53, *59*, 60–6,
    71, 120–1, 196
        GT, 82–4, 122, 123
        911 2.7-litre, 162–4
Christophorous magazine, 36
Clark, Jim, 51–3, 77 8, 137, *138*
clutch, automatic, 155
clutch cable, repair, 134–6
Colotti, Valerio, *114*, 116, *117*
Coltrin, Peter, 53–7, *100*, 140–1
Connaught Cars Ltd, 27–8
'Continental' model, 36, 67
convoy driving, *98*
cornering, 35, 71, 130–1, 146, 163, 191
cost, 164, 165
Cotton, Mike, 192–3, 195

Daimler-Benz, 13, 14 15, 21
Damen model, 35, 38, 44, 67
demonstrator cars, 122–3, 129–31, 193
Dennis, Ron, 202
dinner service, *40*, 41
DKW cars, 13
Donohue, Mark, 174, 179
doors, lack of, 120–1
driving techniques, 32, 35, 42, 71, 134–6

Elford, Vic, 173
engines: development, 58–61, 127, 160, 170–1, 184
    Carrera, 58–61, 64, 82, 127, 147
    cooling, 187, 198
    mounting, 123–4, 184, 187
    pushrod, 58, 146
    4-cylinder, 195, 197

flat 6-cylinder, 127–8, 145, 146, 153, 161–2
flat 8-cylinder, 89, 170, 171, 184
12-cylinder, 170–1, 184
16-cylinder, 183
1½-litre turbo, 198–200
2-litre, 145, 146, 149
2.2-litre, 160
2.5-litre, 193
2.7-litre, 162–4
3.3-litre, 167– 9
4½-litre 12 cylinder, 170–1, 172
5-litre, 172
917 turbo, 175–7
Eves, Edward, *85*
exhaust system, 73

'family', Porsche, 37–8, 41, 45, 87, 147
Fantuzzi, Merdardo, *118*
Faure, Nick, 161
ferries, 92–4, *102*
1500cc Carrera, 49 51, *65*, 145
1500 Normal, 36, 65
1500 Super, 29, 32, 33–4, 44, 49, 51, 53
550 Spyders, *56*, 60, 73
'flashing', 37–8
Florio, Vincenzo, 87
fly, and the airflow, 140
Ford cars, 128, 129
Foster, Alan, 68
4-cam engine, 48–60
Francis, Alf, *117*
Frankenberg, Richard von, 29–32, 33, 35, 36, 42, *43*, 44, 47
Frazer Nash cars, *61*, 63, 155
Frère, Paul, 167
Friedrichshafen (Germ.), *101*
Fuchs, Karl, *26*

Index

fuel consumption, 154, 193
Fuhrmann, Ernst, 58, 61, 64, 162, 182

Gardner, Frank, 173
gearboxes, 83, 155, 160, 163, 188, 191
gear changing, 134–5, 155, 163
General Motors, 127, 145
German racing, 14, 19–21, 24–7, 197
Germer, Gustav, *26*
Grand Prix racing, 13, 14, 22, 198–202

Hamilton, Maurice, *133*
Hanstein, Huschke von, 59, 82, 83, 87, 122–3, *154*, 157, 175
Harrison, Doug, 53, 55, 57
Harrison, Dr, 33–4
headlamp flashing, 37–8
heating, 126–7
Herrmann, Hans, 59, 60, 87, 173
Hill, Graham, 78, 80, *85*, 87
hill climbs, 69–71, 73, 75–7
Hitler, Adolf, 21, 22
Hohfluh (Swit.), 47, *48*, 55, 140
Holyoak, Geoff, 107, 111, 113
Horch company, 13
horsepower, 33–4
Hurrell, Sid, 68

Ickx, Jacky, *199*
International Porsche Rally, 121
Italian racing, 22
Italy, travel, 91–3, *104–5*

Jaguar cars, 147, 151–2, 153, 155–6, 163
Juhan, Jaroslav, 60
Karlskoga race, 106–7

Kinnunen, Leo, 89
Komenda, Irwin, 202

Lancia cars, 29, *30*, 32, *114*
Lauda, Niki, 129
Le Mans races, 173, 197–8, *199*
Linge, Herbert, 60, 80, 82, 83, 173
Loens, André, 107, 108, 111, 113
Lotus Europa, *154*, 157
Lush, Tom, 32

McLaren, Bruce, 202
McLaren Grand Prix car, 198, *199*, 200–2
Mahle, Eberhard, 82
Malaya Garages, 195
manual, driver's, 36–7
Marko, Helmut, 173
Marlboro sponsorship, 198, *199*
Martini Team Replica, 164–5
Maserati cars, 13
Mass, Jochen, 129–31, *133*
Masuy, Marcel, *25*, 27
Mathe, Otto, 24
Mazda cars, 155–6
Mercedes–Benz, 15, 106, 108–9, *112*
Messina ferry, 92–3
Mexican Road Race, 60, 61
'Mickey Mouse', *43*, 44
Mille Miglia race, 22, 45, 65
   1954, 59–60
   1955, 47
   1957, 53–5
Miller, Akton (Uncle Ak), 53, *54*, 55, 56–7
Mimmler, Hubert, 79–80, 132, 179–82
Mitchell, Nancy, 32

modifications, 73–4, 115, *143*
Monte Carlo rallies, 126–7
Monte Cassino, *99*
Montero, Luis, *100*
Monza Grand Prix, 47, 173–4
Moss, Stirling, *56*
motorcycling, 25, 27, 134, 164
Motor Sport, 27, 29, 154
motorway driving, 74–5, 144
mountain driving, 94
Mussolini, Benito, 22

night driving, 34
901 model, 145–6, *149*, 159
904 model, 123–8, 184
907 model, 184
908 model, 87–9, 171
911 series, *60*, 126, 127–8, 146–57, 158, 159, 187, 188
911L, *150,152*
911S, 160–1, *167*
2.7-litre, 162–4, 164
3-litre, *161*, 164, 167, 168
3.3-litre, 167–9
competition cars, 159–60
development, 159–62, 164, 169
turbo, *150*, 153, 164, 165–6, 167, 191, 195–6
912 model, 157
914 model, 156, 157–8
917 model, 170–83, 184
924 model, *185*, 186, 188, 195
928 model, 66, 167, 187–8, 188–91, 195
935 Turbo, 65, 129–31
944 model, 66, 167, *186*, 192–5, 197, *201*
956 model, 24, 198, *199*
noise, 120–1, 125, 153, 165
Nuvolari, Tazio, 19
Nye, Doug, 9, 168

over-steer, 32

parking, *97,103*
parties, 107–8
Pascoe, Tommy, 53
Penske, Roger, 174
Pertwee, Jon, 63, 64
petrol consumption, 154, 193
petrol pump, 64
Peugeot cars, 146
Piëch, Ferdinand, 170, 186
Piper, David, 173
pistons, 155–6
Planfoy hill climb, 29, *30*
plates, commemorative, *40*, 41, 72–3
police cars, 37–8, 39
Porsche Cars Great Britain Ltd, 155, 164, 190, 192, *200*
Porsche Club of America, 121–3
Porsche Engineering, 156, 165, 166–7, 168, 169, 170, 182, 189, 197
origins, 22–4, 27, 28, 32, 187, 202
Porsche, Ferdinand, 13, 14, 15, *16*, 17–18, 19, 21, 23, 24, 198, 202
Porsche, Ferry, *17*, 21, 23, 24, 42, 58, 153, 169, 170, *200*, 200
Portman, Eddy, 77, 78
Potter, Leonard, 68
power, 151, 152, 165–6, 168, 174
public relations, 35–6, 38–41
Pucci, Antonio, 82, 83
push–rod engine, 58, 146
P-wagen, 13–21
Rabe, Karl, 41, 58, 202

Index

racing cars, 13–14, 79, 87, 120–1, 128–9, 159, 197–8
rallying, 66
Redman, Brian, 88, 89
reliability, 84–7
repairs, 49, *110*, 111, *119*, 132–6, 141–4
Reutter seats, 34, 148
rev-counters, 44, 121, 149–51, 161, 165
Riley, Peter, 68
Rodriguez, Pedro, 89, 173
Roebuck, Nigel, *133*
Rome–Berlin race 1939, 22, 23
Rosemeyer, Bernd, 15, 17, *18*,19
Rossi, Gregorio, Count, 183
Rothmans sponsorship, 198, *199*
RSK Spyder, *122*, 123
RS60 Spyder, 79, *80*
rubbing strip, 51, *103*, *193*
running-in, 162–3

safety, 166–7, 177, 181–2
sales, 35–6, 38–41, *105*
Scandinavian travels, 106–13
Scott-Watson, Ian, 51, 53, 77, 137
seat belts, 131
Sebring exhaust, 73
Seidel, Wolfgang, 87
750 Motor Club, 49, 67
Sicily, 79, 91–4, *95–6*
Siffert, Joseph, 88, 89, 173
Silverstone, 49, 51–3, 67–8, 197
single-seater Porsche, *114*, 115–116
Six Hour Relay Race, 49, 51–3, 67–8, 71, 77–8, 136, 197
1600 Super, 51, 65, 71, 75–7, 121, *138*, 145
size, 27, 32, 89, 146, 162

Sloniger, Jerry, 175
snow driving, 42
Solitude circuit, 121, *122*, 146
souvenirs, 36, *40*, 41
speed, 34, 44, 71–2, 74, 121, 166
Speedster model, *36*, *37*, *38*, 53
Sportomatic transmission, 149, *150*, 155
sprints, 69, 73, 74
Spyder model, *31*, 44, *56*, 59–60, 73, 79, 80, *122*, 123
standing starts, 71
starting, gravity, 135
Staniforth, Alan, 68
steering column, 115
Stoop, Dickie, 124–5,*126*, 128
Storez, Claude, 53
Strahle, Paul, 80, 82, 83
styling, 188, 190, 191
suspension, 123, 163, 196
Sweden, driving in, 106–11

'taking off', 71–2
Targa Florio race, 65, 79–80, 94, 120, 157, 159
Taylor, Denis, 68
Techniques d'Avant Garde (TAG), 198
testing, 175 – 82
356 series, 24, 27, *28*, 44, 71, 134, 139, 145, 146, 153, 154, 169
356A, 34, 35–6, 48, *103*, *143*, 145, 147, *201*
356A/1500 GS (Carrera), 61
356B, *46*, *57*, *103*, 134–6, 145, 154
356C, *105*, 145
Super 75, 145
Super 90, 145, 154
towing, 63–4, 142–4

train ferries, *102*
transmission, 155
transporters, *86, 102, 116*
Trengwainton (Cornw.), 71
Trips, Wolfgang Graf Berghe von, 45, 47, 49, 106–13
Triumph TR2, 51–3, 69
turbocharged models, 65, 128, 129, 153, 165–6, 167–9, 175, 188
Tyrrell, Ken, 107

umbrella, souvenir, 36
urban cycle tests, 177–8

V6 engine, 198
V8 engine, 56–7, 188, 197
Vieullet, Auguste, 53
Villeneuve, Gilles, 17
Volkswagen, 19, *20*, 21, 22–3, 58, 154, 157, 198

VW-Porsche, 157–8, 184

Wadsworth, Edgar, 68
Walker, Ian, 68
Wanderer company, 13
weight, 73–4
Weissach research centre, 174–82, 185–6, 189, 197, *198*
wheels, *84, 160, 187, 189*
Whitmore, Sir John, 128, 129
Wilder, Steve, 49, 51, 53, 67, 69, 71, 74–5, 132 4, 136
Windsor, Peter, *133*
wischening, 32, 35, 37–8, 49, 121
Wiscombe Park (Dev.), 74, 75
Woolf, John, 173
Wutherich, Rolf, 126
Wyer, John, 173–4

Zuffenhausen, 34, 35, *105, 127,* 170